AMERICAN TENANT

Everything U Need to Know...™

about

YOUR RIGHTS AS A RENTER

TREVOR RHODES, CEO OF AMERUSA

New York   Chicago   San Francisco   Lisbon
London   Madrid   Mexico City   Milan   New Delhi
San Juan   Seoul   Singapore   Sydney   Toronto

1 2 3 4 5 6 7 8 9 0   FGR/FGR   0 1 4 3 2 1 0 9 8

ISBN-13: P/N 978-0-07-159053-2 of set
                978-0-07-159050-1

ISBN-10: P/N 0-07-159053-6 of set
                0-07-159050-1

Trademarks: EUNTK, EUNTK.com, Everything U Need to Know… and the Everything U Need to Know… horseshoe bar logo are all trademarks of the EUNTK Corporation and may not be used without written permission. All other trademarks are the property of their respective owners.

Disclaimer: While the publisher and the author have used their best efforts in preparing this book, they make no representations or warranties with respect to the accuracy or completeness of the contents. Neither the publisher nor author shall be liable for any loss of profit or commercial damages, including but not limited to, special, incidental, consequential or other damages. If legal advice or other expert assistance is required, it is strongly recommended that the services of a competent and experienced professional should be sought.

McGraw-Hill books are available at special quantity discounts to use as premiums and sales promotions, or for use in corporate training programs. To contact a representative, please visit the Contact Us pages at www.mhprofessional.com.

For information about any of the other Everything U Need to Know… products and services, visit www.EUNTK.com. If you have questions or comments, please email them to feedback@euntk.com.

McGraw-Hill Director, Business Editorial: Mary Glenn
EUNTK Managing Editor: Tomas Mureika
CD-ROM Software: TailoredApplication.com
Index: ProfessionalIndexing.com

This book is printed on acid-free paper.

Library of Congress Cataloging-in-Publication Data

Rhodes, Trevor.
    American tenant : everything U need to know-- about your rights as a renter / By Trevor Rhodes. -- 1st ed.
            p. cm.
    ISBN 0-07-159050-1 (alk. paper)
  1. Landlord and Tenant--United States--Popular works. I. Title.
  KF590.Z9R47 2008
  346.7304'34--dc22

                                                                            2008022909

To those who continue to try their best—

Acknowledgments

This *American Tenant* volume from **Everything U Need to Know... (EUNTK)** would not be possible without the support and assistance from the following companies and individuals: AmerUSA.net, Pamela Phillips, PREMIS (Professional Real Estate Management and Investment Services), and Rhodes Property Management.

Table of Contents

Introduction

You'd think that becoming (or being) a tenant would be such a simple task. You look for a place that's available for rent, you sign a rental agreement and you pay your rent once a month until you decide to leave.

For many, this may be the easiest of tasks. However, **landlord actions, lease agreements** and **rental property conditions** *are not always favorable.* And depending on the laws of your state (and local community), you may be faced with quite an unpleasant experience of having to defend your rights as a renter should there ever be a dispute (and there's usually at least one at some point in time or another). **The key to a successful landlord-tenant relationship** *is not just knowing about what to do* **when you and your landlord disagree, but knowing how to** *prevent* **these legal entanglements from ever occurring** in the first place.

American Tenant is meant to **simplify** and **clarify the complexities** of dealing with issues such as *security deposit deductions, lease agreement violations, landlord acts of discrimination, renting with pets* and *much, much more.* Consider this to be your **comforting guidebook to understanding your rights and responsibilities as an American Tenant.**

Don't worry – as dry as this topic can sometimes be – we've done our best to keep it stimulating, interesting, rewarding and educational throughout this book. Whether this is your first time renting or you're a seasoned tenant, you'll enjoy the light-hearted – yet extremely useful – approach to learning. And if you need further assistance, check out the official website for this entire series at **www.EUNTK.com** – for discussion groups, laws and statutes, other subjects in the series, plus a whole lot more... for the absolute easiest way there is to learn **"Everything U Need to Know..."**

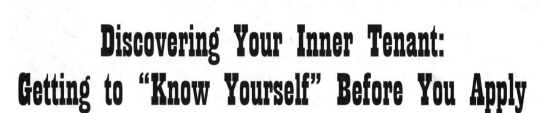

Chapter 1

Discovering Your Inner Tenant:
Getting to "Know Yourself" Before You Apply

This Chapter Discusses:

★ **The Landlord-Tenant Relationship**
★ **Consumer Credit Reports**
★ **Criminal Records**
★ **Evictions Records**

Stop! Before you even begin thinking about looking (let alone applying) for a place to rent, you need to **be sure that you are prepared to open yourself up to the highest levels of scrutiny**. Failing to prepare yourself could easily jeopardize your chances of getting a favorable lease or – as is the case with so many – *any* lease at all.

You often hear the phrase: **"Honesty is the best policy"** – but landlords seldom get a chance to experience this first-hand. Believe it or not, **landlords *do* appreciate honesty** – maybe more than the ordinary Joe. After all, many landlords have thousands of dollars or more invested in real estate, which they must protect – and **they are looking to rent that property to someone who they feel can be trusted with such a valuable asset for several months or years.**

The Landlord-Tenant Relationship

The single most important thing you will read in this *American Tenant* volume **is the following: The relationship between a landlord and a tenant is the most critical element in any successful leasing agreement!** This also applies to partnerships, friendships and marriages – **an open and honest communication is indisputably** *the* **most important factor in having a long and successful relationship**, no matter who you are or whom it is with. When it comes to being a tenant, if you maintain this type of honest and reliable relationship with your landlord, *you will be amazed by how much leeway you are given and the many liberties your landlord will allow you*.

However, as with any good thing in life, this type of relationship is not automatically going to come your way and **must be diligently earned**.

EXAMPLE

A landlord who doesn't trust you won't be as lenient or understanding on what are serious issues to you – such as having to make a late rental payment or making an exception to an otherwise-stated rule (e.g., accepting your pet, in spite of general policy *not* to do so).

What is critical to know – and the reason *why American Tenant* is giving you the single most valuable piece of advice right away – is that **the landlord-tenant relationship begins the moment you first speak to a potential landlord, look at the property and fill out the rental application**.

In all your talks with your potential new landlord – and especially in what you "say" on your rental application – **you will be demonstrating and representing significant things about yourself** that will create that ever-invaluable *"first impression."* If you establish your relationship on a basis of **openness**, **honesty** and **reliability** (i.e., *you actually follow through on what you say you're going to do!*), it will lead the landlord into trusting you... and **Yee-hah!** *Your new leasing experience has just been improved exponentially before you've even paid a dime.*

Sure, this may seem like stating the overly obvious, but – again – this is precisely *why* this volume begins with this one piece of advice – *because it truly cannot be stressed enough*. And **the first step in this process is "getting to know yourself"** – not in any psychoanalytical fashion, but **who you are as an** *American Tenant*.

It is important to become aware of how you are presenting yourself to potential landlords *from the outset.*

Has your personal *credit taken its share of bullets*? Do you have a *criminal record trailing you* from your distant past? Have you ever been *evicted*? These are questions that **may seem like deal-breakers** and may lower your "self-esteem" as a would-be tenant – but, cheer up, buckaroo! In the next few sections, you'll learn how to deal with those issues and make that paramount landlord-tenant relationship work to your advantage. **Things are never insurmountable –** *provided you keep your dealings with your landlord both professional and congenial.*

<u>For example</u>: Let's start with the issue that's affected most tenants' lives at some point or another: The dreaded *personal credit report*!

Consumer Credit Reports

This is it! – The **consumer credit report** is **the single, most universally utilized tool to screen a tenant** *anywhere in the United States*. In fact, *the overwhelming majority of creditors* in general (e.g., banks, lenders, credit card companies, landlords, etc.) *use one every time someone applies*. So **in case you're like most people and haven't been regularly monitoring your personal credit report** – and you've kept getting turned down or getting the highest interest rate anytime you apply for something, then **you need to find out what's on your credit report today!**

That's right – ***there's no reason to wait!*** In fact, the longer you wait (for those that have bad credit), the longer you will continue to be penalized for something that ***may very well be reversible.***

Log on to any computer connected to the Internet and get your free copy within seconds – there are no gimmicks or costly subscriptions required to exercise your right under the **U.S. FACT Act**. Therefore, don't be derailed into paying one dime to find out exactly what's on your credit report once a year.

Visit: **www.AnnualCreditReport.com** to see exactly what information is being reported about you from ***all three of the major credit bureaus***: **Equifax**, **Experian** and **TransUnion**. You should plan on doing this ***annually*** – for both your own protection ***and*** benefit. Not only will you be able to see unauthorized accounts or inquiries made by **identity thieves**, but you'll also know whether or not your creditors are accurately reporting information about your financial obligations and their respective payment histories.

There are many ways to approach repairing your credit report; just a few have been highlighted on the next two pages. For a more in-depth analysis and step-by-step instructions on how to repair your credit – and essentially beat the system – check out the ***American Credit Repair*** **volume** in the **"Everything You Need to Know…"** **series**. ***American Credit Repair*** is the ultimate "one-stop, do-it-yourself" **credit repair guide**, completely equipped with sets of forms, letters and more on an **accompanying CD-ROM**. ***Don't bother hiring dubious credit repair companies*** when the law allows you to take care of your own business without wasting anymore of your hard earned money.

> ### *I found something on my credit report – what do I do?*

If you found either erroneous or fraudulent information, *you have every right to dispute your file online and have the problem investigated*. Count on it taking **30 days** for the dispute process to run its course. The results of the investigation will then be mailed to you upon completion.

> ### *Should I pay off an old account that has already been assigned to a collection agency?*

The only way it is *ever* suggested that you pay an outstanding collection account is *to get the collection agency to agree to completely remove any and all information pertaining to the account from the credit bureaus in exchange for a full and final payment* – needless to say, this should be agreed upon in writing. Now if the agency doesn't want to agree to this, here is something to think about: **The Fair Credit Reporting Act (FCRA)** *only allows an outstanding creditor obligation* (such as a collection account) *to remain on a consumer's file for no more than seven years from the last date of activity* (e.g., a payment or credit being initiated by the consumer). So – hypothetically – *if you never make a payment, the account will eventually be removed from your credit file as if it never existed*. Interesting, huh?

> ### *Okay, but I need to move in the next couple of weeks... What can I do to immediately improve my credit rating?*

There are actually several things you can do, but only one of them is recommended and practical at this point – the others would require a lengthy dissertation on how to repair your credit, which can barely be shoehorned into its own separate *"Everything You Need to Know..."* **volume**.

However, without getting into sophisticated negotiation techniques and repair tactics to achieve a favorable account rating, this more practical approach can be accomplished by everyone.

It doesn't matter what type of negative payment history you have on your personal credit report. Whatever it may be, there is an easy way to handle it – as simple as this may sound, you must do the following:

♦ Before applying for a place to rent, you must first *obtain the most recent copy of your credit report*. If you haven't already done so, **get all three for free** at **www.AnnualCreditReport.com** – or, if you have already received your free copies in the past year, then visit **www.CreditReportRepair.com** to pay for access to all three credit bureaus. Don't worry – every time you pull your own credit report through either service, it doesn't count as a hit against your credit rating. The only unfortunate thing is that if you already took advantage of your rights under the **FACT Act** for this year, you're now forced to pay a fee in order to view the most recent version.

♦ After receiving the latest copy of all three credit reports, you must **make a list of every derogatory account that appears on your record** – whether it's late payments, collections, or whatever.

♦ Okay, this is it! This is where you can **make your amends (at least to your prospective landlord)**. No snake oil or dog and pony show required – *All you need to do is prepare a letter* (don't worry – nothing too formal, but **definitely** sincere) which *openly discloses every derogatory account* you have, *the reason why the negative remark occurred* and *what steps you have taken (or are taking) to correct the problem*.

Sure, it may seem a little ridiculous and simplistic… *but it works!*

Regardless of whatever may have you so anxious and worried, **the majority of landlords really do appreciate when their potential tenants are open, honest and sincere, especially about all of the bad stuff**.

Landlords hate nothing more than accepting a rental application, only later to discover that the prospective tenant's meager admission of "minor credit problems" actually meant *a heck* of a lot more! *Show the landlord that you are aware of your mistakes* – *even* though there is always that possibility that the landlord may not pull your credit report – and yes, believe it or not, there are still a few landlords out there that don't bother to run a credit check. But I wouldn't bet the bank on it!

So don't dismiss this tactic! Chances are, you've probably never tried it and you'll be surprised **how effective it can be – *on many different levels*.** Of course, there are never any guarantees, but most of the time you should be approved – though perhaps with additional contingencies (e.g. a little extra security deposit). But at least you got exactly what you wanted – a new place to settle your 'stead.

Criminal Records

It's a given that *some crimes are just not easily forgiven* – even for those landlords that profess to be devoutly religious. But unless you've committed one of those heinous acts that are so recurrent in the media headlines, the vast majority of criminal records can be *handled with dignity and confidence* – after all, many more *American Tenants* than you'd think have broken the law, which can be easily explained *and* forgiven.

Depending on the time frame with which you have to work, **the best way to deal with any criminal conviction is to seek an "expungement."** An *expungement* is a legal process whereby the sentencing court – upon your formal request – agrees to alter the permanent record to appear less severe. **The nature of the expungement *depends on whether you were a juvenile or an adult at the time of the conviction*,** whether it was a *felony or misdemeanor* offense and the *sentence you received* (e.g., probation, jail time, prison term, etc.).

In order to get your record expunged, you will need an attorney to file a motion with the court. But before you make the effort to initiate the process, make sure you have lived as a mindfully law-abiding citizen *since* the conviction. Many judges will naturally deny your request if you've kept up the life of an outlaw – or even just made a few additional mistakes here and there.

So **don't bother wasting the court's time and your money if you're still continuing to get into legal trouble periodically.** Your best approach then would be to *stop your bad habits* and *spill the beans to your would-be landlord, as recommended in the following option...*

If you don't have a lot of time or the resources necessary to have your record expunged, then you have the same alternative explained in the consumer credit report section. You must take the time to *formally explain the conviction, when it occurred, the reason why and how you may have changed and/or learned from the incident.*

In addition to your explanation, **it also helps to include letters of recommendation** from your friends, family, past or present employers – even your probation officer (if applicable) – which should serve to attest to your overall character and integrity. *The letters should ideally also openly acknowledge your conviction for a better legal life thereafter.* Certainly, any associations or religious or nonprofit organizations of which you are a member or with which you are at least affiliated can prove very important to establishing your current credibility.

Obviously, the extent to which you need to use every weapon in your arsenal just to appease your prospective landlord will be contingent upon the severity of your individual offense. The fiercer the crime, the more you need to counter it with resounding praise and support.

Remember: Your prospective landlord doesn't know you – and, initially, has *no* reason to trust you. **This is your *only* chance to make the landlord believe that – despite possible evidence to the contrary – you *will* be a good, law-abiding tenant.**

Eviction Records

An applicant who brings a prior eviction to the table is –
as you would expect – looked at differently from the "bad
credit consumer" or "convicted felon." Despite having
paid a few bills late or trespassed a few too many times,
an eviction (to the contrary) **says you have caused a
previous landlord financial and emotional distress –**
it takes money and time to have someone forcibly removed from a rental property.

Unfortunately, **it's rare to have an eviction record removed (or expunged).** The
best time to fight an eviction is at the time of the original court proceedings when you
are given a chance to present your side of the story to the judge. Otherwise, you'll
need to do a really good job at convincing the court why you are entitled to have your
record expunged.

 So what can you do about an eviction record?

> **For one**: If there is any money still owed to your previous landlord
> (usually in the form of a monetary judgment awarded by the court),
> you should consider paying it off – to at least have the record marked
> as **"satisfied." This effort will show that – despite the relationship
> going sour – you still had the temperament to make good on an
> outstanding bad debt.** That, by itself, *almost* says enough to have
> the new landlord lean toward forgetting all about the previous
> eviction altogether.
>
> If you are unable to afford to pay your outstanding obligation –
> or perhaps no money was ever owed as a part of the court's ruling –
> then your best bet (again) is to be proactive by being *up front with
> the new landlord before he or she finds out about your past*.

Remember: Your attitude and tone while communicating these explanations say as
much as the words coming out of your mouth – if not more so!

Aside from the far greater tasks of performing your own extensive credit repair or an attorney-assisted record cleansing, **there is nothing better than the persuasive power of the truth**. Landlords possess that same human quality that other human beings do – so, just like us, they usually know full well when they're being treated with respect, as opposed to being played like a fiddle.

This strategy may not work 100% of the time – but it should prove successful the vast majority of the time. It's all in the **openness**, **honesty** and **reliability** you present to your would-be landlord. Later chapters will discuss the importance of keeping these trustworthy values at full force to ensure you have the best possible tenancy. Sure, there will always be those difficult folks that want nothing more than to make your stay as unpleasant as possible – but **most legitimate landlords truly welcome the prospect of this being a truly positive experience for both of you!**

Chapter 2

Renting 101:
Looking for a Place to Live

This Chapter Discusses:

★ **Where to Look**
★ **Functional, Not Fanciful**
★ **Budgeting Yourself**
★ **Location, Location, Location**
★ **House Vs. Apartment**

This is exciting! – At least, it is for those just turning 18 and venturing out on their own or for those seasoned adults that are moving to a new area. Looking for a new place to live (or maybe your very first place to live on your own) shouldn't be another headache in the daily grind of life (unless you were understandably forced to become a tenant because you lost your home due to foreclosure – that's a whole different story). **With today's surplus of rental inventory from sluggish real estate sales, you should be able to find exactly what you need and get a great deal.**

Where to Look

As if you need to be told, right? **Rentals are everywhere.**
The important thing to note for this section is that *it's not
necessary to pay to find a place to live.* There are several
lists you can buy and agencies you can hire, but these are
absolutely unnecessary – especially with today's rental inventory
surplus. **Don't be coaxed into having to pay anyone to lead you to any special
deals – because they're out there for everyone to partake; it just takes a little
effort on your part to find them.**

So where do you start looking? **Here is a list of the most common ways to search...**

Tips on Where to Find a Place to Rent:

☆ Internet

Almost everyone is online today; even those in the most remote
valleys and hilltops can seem to get access, especially with mobile
Internet connections. **There appears to be an endless list of rental
property listings, roommate services, subletting websites and
vacation rentals available here.** To view the latest and greatest of
websites for tenants, *visit* **EUNTK.com.**

☆ Newspapers

The **classifieds section of the newspaper is still a great source for
rental property.** *There is one downside, however,* for those who are
looking for a lower priced unit in heavily circulated newspapers
(100,000+ subscribers), because **the cost of the ad may not be
worth the effort for lower rent landlords unless it is a multi-unit
apartment complex.** *Smaller local newspapers*, on the other hand,
offer not only **affordable advertising for landlords,** but also **usually
a more targeted search area for tenants.**

 Real Estate Agents

There are **two types of real estate agents that can help you.** The first is *one who operates a property management business.* These agents are licensed professionals that represent rental property owners to ensure the unit is marketed when vacant and looked after when occupied. The real estate agent usually charges a recurring percentage of the rent to the property owner (10% on average). **Fortunately, there is no cost to you – except these agents may charge you an application fee** ($25 to $35 in most areas) **to cover their tenant screening costs** (i.e., for a credit report, criminal background check and/or an eviction search).

The **second type** is referred to as **a tenant placement agent.** These real estate agents **generally don't do many sales** – *their money is made by receiving a commission if they are able to bring a qualified tenant to a landlord.* Once again, **there is no cost to you to have them find you a place to rent.** *However, you may have to pay a minimal application fee to apply.* The landlord usually compensates the agent anywhere from a few hundred dollars all the way up to the equivalent of an entire month's rent if you qualify and execute a lease agreement.

Functional, Not Fanciful

For most tenants, renting is only temporary – with homeownership being the goal. If you share the same thought, then **you should be careful about the money you spend on your monthly rent.** After all, **there is no equity, significant tax advantages or real benefit from paying rent** – other than the fact that you don't have to pay for the taxes and insurance and your payment may be less than a mortgage, which gives you instant expendable cash.

The point of this section is to remind you (unless it's your destiny to rent for the rest of your life) that **cash management is critical in order to accumulate a significant savings account.** Before you move into the three-bedroom unit (when you only need two) or pay the extra premium for the view of a reservoir pond, *ask yourself if the additional expense is really necessary.*

If you're new to renting, **you may not appreciate the cash management aspect of this section until you've rented for 20 years and then realize that you've spent thousands** *(if not hundreds of thousands)* **of dollars and have nothing to show for it except for time spent living in a place that is not yours to keep.**

This is why *functional outweighs fanciful.* **Find a modest place to rent that provides the security and comfort you need while transitioning into a home that you own.** And for the few of you that prefer to rent (or the many that cannot afford to buy) in the area where you prefer to live – like southern California residents – then **cope as best as you can.**

Southern California is a good example, because along the coastline is the greatest weather in the world. As soon as you begin to move inland, the climate dries up and heats up. Unfortunately, the closer you get to the coastline (such as Venice Beach), the more expensive real estate becomes; a 900-square foot two-bedroom house with enough land around it to barely keep the ants happy sold for about $550,000 in 2007. By the way, that's for a house built 40+ years ago with only one bathroom and no air conditioning. So you can see why some may be inclined to rent instead. **The same type of unit could be rented for only $1,500 per month, which is a breath of fresh air as opposed to trying to manage a $3,500 mortgage payment.**

Obviously, your local circumstances will dictate what you do. **With the current state of the U.S. economy, you should consider making better use of any extra money you may have instead of giving it to your landlord.**

Budgeting Yourself

This picks up from the previous section, but steers the focus to **specific budgeting issues**, regardless of whether you rent or own your home. Small things add up quickly. So, **when you sit down to determine what you can afford to pay each month, don't forget to allow for the incidentals,** such as cable TV, telephone, utilities and other residential expenses like doing your laundry.

At this point, a blank sheet of paper and a pencil would do just fine to hammer out the details of what you can afford to pay in rent each month. **You don't need a fancy budget worksheet; just sit down and write out what you spend and how often you spend it.** And if it's necessary, **take the time to monitor your cash spending and monthly bills so you can record a more accurate accounting.** *Just be sure to make a note of each item and the frequency at which it occurs.*

One of the most important reminders common throughout this series is **to not forget about setting aside money for your retirement.** Whether it's a **401(k), IRA** or **savings account,** *you should be setting aside at least 10% of your monthly income.* Now, this may be difficult for some and that's understood – but **as soon as times get better, do your best to catch up.** If you've been paying attention to the news media, then you know that **social security checks and Medicare may not be there when you retire.**

Location, Location, Location

Picking the right location in which to live (even if it's just a short-term stay) **can add years to your life and dollars to your pocket.** It's just a simple matter of determining what's important to you. **Here is a basic list of what to consider when scouting a location...**

Things to Consider When Choosing a Location:

★ Employment

Avoiding a stressfully long commute and daily traffic congestion can add years to your life and a little extra money in your pocket just from the gasoline savings, not to mention the advantages of maintaining lower vehicle mileage. Being close to your job definitely has its benefits – unless you work at a plutonium enrichment facility or sewage treatment plant; then you might want to live as far away as possible from the smell and toxic waste.

★ Public Transportation

This isn't just for those that do not have cars; **many public transit systems** (especially in the nation's bigger cities, which operate on a railway) **make the daily commute easier and more affordable** for those that do own vehicles. **Something to consider if it's a toss-up between one unit that is near a station or pick-up point versus one that's not.**

★ School District

For those who have children, you should **research area schools to determine where you prefer your children to attend.** There are many statistics available on the Internet that will assist in grading area schools. **Visit EUNTK.com for more information.**

 ### Crime

This is an interesting topic, because real estate professionals and landlords (in fear of violating **Fair Housing Laws**) have to tiptoe around the issue of criminal activity when asked questions about any given area. Therefore, you should **do your own research by contacting the local police or sheriff's department for area statistics.** You can even **visit EUNTK.com for information on how to search criminal statistics.**

 ### Conveniences

Depending on your personal needs and priorities, **living near a grocery store, shopping mall, hospital or place of worship may make life a little easier.** Tenants can get so caught up with the superficial traits of a rental unit or apartment complex amenities, **they tend to forget about the conveniences that an area may offer, even though the rental may not be as plush or new.**

House Vs. Apartment

Besides how many flights of stairs you'll have to climb, **there are pros and cons to whether you should rent a house or an apartment.** While not all circumstances are the same for every house or apartment, **a basic assessment has been provided on the following pages...**

The Advantages of Renting a House:

★ Privacy

There is **no better way to ensure your privacy than to have a detached single-family house that does not share walls, ceilings and floors with your neighbors.**

★ Convenient Parking

Being able to **park in your own driveway (or garage) sure beats a parking garage, carport or the open air** – especially when the weather is bad.

★ Private Yard

Having **room to breathe and an area for your children to play or for you to barbeque** is a plus for some.

★ Larger Space

Houses are typically **more spacious as far as living area and storage.** Depending on how many bedrooms you need or extra rooms for furniture, home office, etc., **a home (even a 2-bedroom home) usually has more living space.**

The Disadvantages of Renting a House:

★ Higher Rent

The **monthly rental amount is usually higher than an apartment** with the same amount of bedrooms.

Higher Utility Bills

Water consumption and electricity usage are typically higher in a house. A house typically has a lawn that needs to be watered, and the extra living space **without having shared walls reduces its energy efficiency.**

★ Yard Maintenance

Depending on the arrangement with the landlord, **many times, you are responsible for maintaining the yard.** This means mowing, watering and trimming it.

The Advantages of Renting an Apartment:

★ Lower Rent

On average, **apartments are less expensive to rent than a house.**

★ Lower Utility Bills

Smaller living areas (especially ones that are insulated by neighboring walls) **tend to be more energy efficient and therefore, less expensive.**

★ Maintenance Free

Whether it's the clubhouse, pool, landscaping or other amenities, **tenants are rarely ever asked to maintain them –** *just not to abuse them.*

The Disadvantages of Renting an Apartment:

★ Lack of Privacy

While you may live behind closed doors, **if you share a wall with your neighbor, chances are you can hear** all of their laughter and arguments just as they can hear yours.

★ Poor Parking

Most apartments do not offer assigned parking – and even if they do, it's usually not sheltered. So you may have to deal with a little walking and foul weather on occasion.

★ Communal Yard

For those that like to sit outside, **you may have to endure some extra foot traffic and company.** *Apartments don't have private yards.* However, **communal recreation centers, pools and tennis courts can often make up for this inadequacy.**

★ Less Space

Even though there are many three-bedroom apartments being constructed today, **they don't come equipped with the extra storage space and living area found in houses.**

Ultimately, **it doesn't matter** *where* **you decide to rent, so long as you're not wasting too much of your money and live in a** *safe and secure area*. Unfortunately, *there are no guarantees of safety* – **even million dollar neighborhoods breed criminals and sex offenders.**

Before You Sign on the Dotted Line, Part I: The Pre-Leasing Tour of the Property

This Chapter Discusses:

★ **What to Look For**
★ **What Questions to Ask**
★ **What to Agree To**
★ **What Not to Agree To**

Just because you found an area and a rental unit you fell in love with, doesn't mean that everything is good to go. This is especially true for those of you that are looking online and are considering going about this sight unseen. *Lease agreements are legally binding contracts* – just like multi-million dollar movie deals and publicly traded corporate mergers. **So before you even apply, you should take a moment to tour the unit and the grounds with the landlord.**

What to Look For

There is an **essential list of items to look for before applying for a rental** and these are **not to be confused with the move-in inspection** discussed in **Chapter 5.** You will most likely have additional concerns or items of interest that need to be included and satisfied before you apply, but **this section will at least serve as a good starting point.** Just be sure you **allow yourself ample time to thoroughly assess everything that's important to you** and *never let the landlord rush you.*

Things to Consider When Touring a Place to Rent:

☆ Signs of Pests and Vermin

Sadly, **even the nicest of places can be infested with little creatures and night crawlers.** This is an important factor to consider with apartment complexes – because if there are other tenants present and the problem still persists, then you'll know how attentive your landlord will be. As far as vacant houses, a few pests may be possible if the unit has been empty for a while. However, it's hard to accept any degree of neglect.

☆ Grounds

Well-maintained/manicured grounds are a good indication of a rental that may have been properly cared for, because the landscaping is usually the first thing a landlord will let go.

☆ Security

Having a secure place to live is obviously essential. This applies to not only the unit, **which should have necessary window and door locks (including deadbolts)**, but the **surrounding area.** Is **vehicular traffic monitored** by an electronic gate or security officer? If not, **contact local law enforcement and ask about crime in the area.**

☆ Hot Water Capacity

Ever rent a unit (or even a hotel for a night) only to discover that **your shower goes cold in five minutes or shortly after someone else takes one?** It may not seem that important in the summer – but just wait for those cold mornings.

☆ Heating and Cooling

A **comfortable living environment** is usually high on the list for most. Regardless of the time of year you are looking, you want to **make sure the climate control system is good enough to keep you and your family happy throughout the year.** *So test it out.*

☆ Noise

Something **seldom thought about, but aggravating** when you (or your child) are repeatedly awakened by sirens in the early morning hours, because your unit is situated next to a busy street. For this reason, **you may want to visit the unit at different times during the day – not just for outside disturbances, but ones coming from neighbors,** if your unit is part of a larger building.

What Questions to Ask

As you are touring the rental, start firing away with your questions. While some of the answers may be coated in corn syrup, **rapid-fire questions may yield some valuable information.** Here is a **suggested list of questions to ask your prospective landlord.** These *should be added to your own personal arsenal of inquiries.*

Everything U Need to Know...

Questions to Ask Your Prospective Landlord:

➤ *Are utilities included?*

This is undoubtedly **the number one concern for most tenants.** It's an important selling point, because **the last thing anyone wants to worry about is another bill.** The most commonly included utility is **water.** However, **electricity, natural gas** and **even cable TV** have been included before.

➤ *Are you responsible for any maintenance or repairs?*

Sometimes landlords (although more often with commercial space) will **require you to maintain and repair the heating and cooling system** or at least take care of **the more common residential maintenance issues** – such as the landscaping, smoke detector batteries and air filters.

➤ *How is trash removed?*

This is usually straightforward for houses, but **there's nothing worse than moving into an apartment only to find out that you have to transport your trash** on Monday morning to the dumpster situated at the front of your complex (usually in your car, eww!). So **find out exactly where and when trash must be removed.**

➤ *Is there assigned parking?*

An **assigned parking space comes in handy when living at a larger complex.** This question may also include **whether there is an additional fee** as well (sometimes encountered in larger cities).

➤ *What is the amount of the rent?*

While you may think you know the rent by the advertised price, **it's always good to clarify** *exactly what* **is being charged for rent when you are face-to-face with the landlord.**

➤ *When is the rent due?*

In addition to how much they are charging for rent, **it's good to know in advance whether the due date for the rent will coincide with your payday.**

➤ *Is there a security deposit?*

As you probably already know, **landlords will charge a standard security deposit** *(usually equivalent to one month's rent)* **to protect against excessive wear and tear.**

➤ *How much does it cost to move in?*

While you asked about the rent and security deposit, **many landlords offer move-in incentives that will better help you to cope with the move.** If not, *now's the time to find out, so you know how much you have to bring to the table.* Some landlords charge the first month's rent, last month's rent and a security deposit. Fortunately, in today's real estate market, *move-in costs can be negotiated.*

➤ *What is the pet policy?*

If you have pets, **you need to know whether the landlord even accepts pets and then of course what size and type.** In addition, you should ask if there is *a refundable or non-refundable pet deposit.* Most landlords will charge **a couple hundred dollars or more** to cover the costs of any potential damage.

Are there laundry facilities?

This is another instance of the obvious – which is sometimes overlooked until after you sign the lease agreement and **realize that the nearest self-service laundry isn't in your unit (or complex) – it's 5 miles away!**

 What type of background check is performed?

This type of knowledge is **useful when trying to establish your character right up front** as discussed in **Chapter 1**. It's better to know what they will be searching for, specifically, **so you can address improprieties.**

What to Agree To

There are certain things (depending on your personal needs) that are **often okay to accept, so long as they are applied to all applicants, so as not to discriminate.** However, *you can decide to walk away at any time.* This section will merely serve as a **basic guide to reasonable expectations of landlords around the country.**

It's Okay for a Landlord to Require the Following:

☆ Method of Payment

A landlord has the right to accept only certain forms of payment. Surprisingly, while most will accept personal checks and money orders, **many will not accept cash.**

☆ Lawn Maintenance

This **usually applies to those renting a detached single-family residence** (e.g., house). It's actually a toss-up: some will ask you to

mow the lawn, while others will prefer to have their same service provider continue to ensure it's kept up.

⭐ Number of Occupants

It's reasonable for a landlord to limit the number of occupants that are living in any given unit.

⭐ Rent Due Date

Unless you have specific needs to accommodate your pay schedule, **it's the landlord's right to say when the rent is due.** After all, the landlord may have a mortgage to pay.

⭐ Pet Policy

Landlords are not required to accept pets and if they choose to, they may establish pet type, size and breed guidelines, so long as the guidelines are consistently upheld (equally) for all tenants.

⭐ Cleaning Fee

Landlords will often disclose that a cleaning fee may be required upon moving out. This is okay, because the fee is **normally imposed only if you didn't bother to clean the unit upon moving out of it.** More on this topic is discussed in **Chapter 8.**

⭐ Utilities

It is generally expected that **you will be required to pay for all utilities** – including natural gas, electric, telephone, cable TV and water. So if the landlord decides to include any of these in your **rent, it's a good thing (unless your rent is adjusted by a stiff premium** for the apparent generosity).

What Not to Agree To

You can choose to fight your own battles, but the following list is **generally accepted as unreasonable expectations of the landlord.**

It's Not Okay for a Landlord to Require the Following:

☆ Property Taxes

For some reason, this story keeps creeping up with **AmerUSA.net** (the nation's leading tenant screening company for individual landlords). **It has been reported that landlords have been requiring tenants to pay for the landlord's own property taxes.** This is – *without question* – **an unreasonable requirement.**

☆ Waste Disposal

Most rental situations **should not require you to pay for waste management services** to dispose of your weekly trash.

☆ Heating and Cooling Maintenance

Aside from changing clogged air filters, **you should never be required to maintain such a considerable expense** as the air condition unit – which is owned by the landlord. In fact, there are areas in the United States where **landlords are required to make sure the heating and cooling systems achieve a certain temperature.** For example: Because of heat waves, Dallas, Texas requires landlords to make sure the air conditioning system can cool the unit to at least 85 degrees.

☆ Plumbing

Unless it's apparent that you broke something, the landlord should be responsible for all plumbing repairs. However, if the

damages are not a result of normal wear and tear and are a **result of tenant abuse, you can be held liable for the cost to repair the damages.** For example, repeatedly clogging the drains with kid's toys is *not* normal wear and tear. On the other hand, gaskets needing to be replaced to prevent a faucet from dripping *would* be considered normal wear and tear.

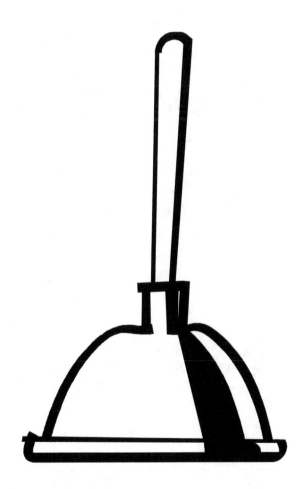

Chapter 4

Before You Sign on the Dotted Line, Part II: Negotiating a Lease Agreement

This Chapter Discusses:

★ **A Sample Lease Agreement**

★ **Understanding Each Clause**

★ **How to Negotiate Your List of Demands**

After you've toured the rental and bombarded the landlord with all of your questions, it's time to negotiate the terms of your tenancy. *Don't think that just because a landlord has his or her own proprietary lease or office supply store template that you must accept everything that is being presented to you.* To the contrary, **all contracts (such as a lease agreement) can be negotiated** – maybe not entirely in your favor, but **there's usually some wiggle room worth exploiting.**

A Sample Lease Agreement

A **sample of a residential lease has been provided on the next four pages** to serve as basic guide for this chapter. While the premise behind every rental agreement is essentially the same, your landlord will undoubtedly use a different one – so **don't assume you will see identical terms and conditions throughout.**

This agreement is **first presented to you in its entirety** and then **broken down (by clause) in the next section,** so you can **understand the purpose of each part and the impact it may have on you.** The more you know, the more empowered you will be – especially since *lease agreements are primarily for the protection of the landlord.*

Lease Agreement

Instructions:
1. Insert your IMAGE or LOGO (optional)
2. Highlight & complete LEASE AGREEMENT FIELDS
3. REPLACE ALL of this text with YOUR contact info
4. Click on 'PRINT FORM' when finished

Everything U Need to Know...

Click here to insert image/logo

Residential Lease Agreement

AGREEMENT TO LEASE

This agreement is entered into between _____ , of
_____ , _____ , referred to as "lessor," and _____ , of
_____ , _____ County,
_____ , referred to as "lessee."

RECITALS

A. Lessor is the owner and/or manager of real property that is available for lease.

B. Lessee desires to lease residential property to occupy and use as their residence.

C. The parties desire to establish an agreement to ensure a future lease of the residential property described in this agreement.

In consideration of the matters described above, and of the mutual benefits and obligations set forth in this agreement, the parties agree as follows:

SECTION I - SUBJECT OF LEASE

Lessor shall lease to prospective lessee the residential property owned by prospective lessor located at
_____ , _____ , _____ County,
_____ , for lessee and their family to occupy and use as their residence.

SECTION II - TERM OF LEASE

The premises shall be leased to lessee for a period of _____ starting from
_____ . Any option to renew, extend or modify this lease shall require the approval of both the lessee and lessor.

SECTION III - MONTHLY RENTAL

Lessee shall pay $ _____ per month as the monthly rental for the term of the lease with the first payment due on or before _____ , and subsequent payments on the _____ day of each succeeding month. This rental payment shall be subject to renegotiation by the parties at any time either of the parties exercises the option to renew the lease under the provisions of any subsequent lease agreement. It is agreed that if the rental payment is not received by the _____ day of the month, then a late fee of _____ shall be assessed and due immediately. Additional terms: _____
_____

SECTION IV - SECURITY DEPOSIT

On the execution of this lease, lessee deposits with lessor $ _____ , receipt of which is acknowledged by lessor, as security for the faithful performance by lessee of the terms of this lease agreement, to be returned to lessee, without interest (unless required by law), on the full and faithful performance by lessee of the provisions of this residential lease agreement.

SAMPLE

Everything U Need to Know...

Lease Agreement

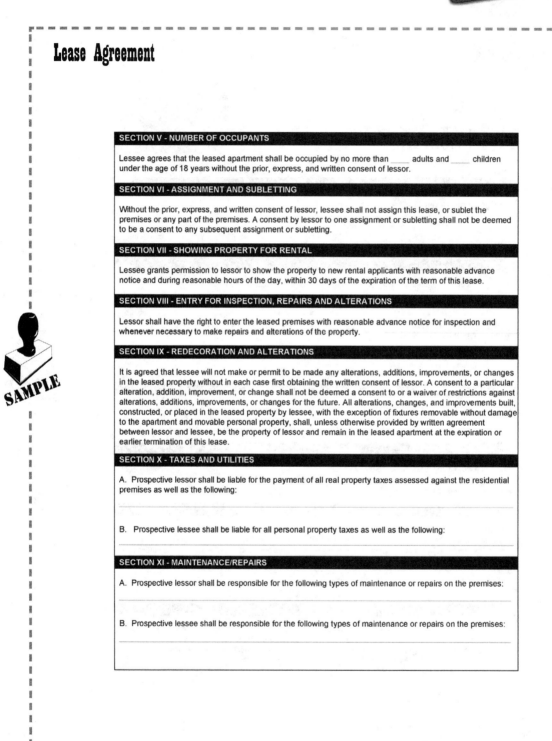

SECTION V - NUMBER OF OCCUPANTS

Lessee agrees that the leased apartment shall be occupied by no more than _____ adults and _____ children under the age of 18 years without the prior, express, and written consent of lessor.

SECTION VI - ASSIGNMENT AND SUBLETTING

Without the prior, express, and written consent of lessor, lessee shall not assign this lease, or sublet the premises or any part of the premises. A consent by lessor to one assignment or subletting shall not be deemed to be a consent to any subsequent assignment or subletting.

SECTION VII - SHOWING PROPERTY FOR RENTAL

Lessee grants permission to lessor to show the property to new rental applicants with reasonable advance notice and during reasonable hours of the day, within 30 days of the expiration of the term of this lease.

SECTION VIII - ENTRY FOR INSPECTION, REPAIRS AND ALTERATIONS

Lessor shall have the right to enter the leased premises with reasonable advance notice for inspection and whenever necessary to make repairs and alterations of the property.

SECTION IX - REDECORATION AND ALTERATIONS

It is agreed that lessee will not make or permit to be made any alterations, additions, improvements, or changes in the leased property without in each case first obtaining the written consent of lessor. A consent to a particular alteration, addition, improvement, or change shall not be deemed a consent to or a waiver of restrictions against alterations, additions, improvements, or changes for the future. All alterations, changes, and improvements built, constructed, or placed in the leased property by lessee, with the exception of fixtures removable without damage to the apartment and movable personal property, shall, unless otherwise provided by written agreement between lessor and lessee, be the property of lessor and remain in the leased apartment at the expiration or earlier termination of this lease.

SECTION X - TAXES AND UTILITIES

A. Prospective lessor shall be liable for the payment of all real property taxes assessed against the residential premises as well as the following:

_____

B. Prospective lessee shall be liable for all personal property taxes as well as the following:

_____

SECTION XI - MAINTENANCE/REPAIRS

A. Prospective lessor shall be responsible for the following types of maintenance or repairs on the premises:

_____

B. Prospective lessee shall be responsible for the following types of maintenance or repairs on the premises:

_____

SAMPLE

Lease Agreement

SECTION XII - ANIMALS

Lessee shall keep no domestic or other animals in or about the property or on the property premises without the prior, express, and written consent of lessor.

SECTION XIII - WASTE, NUISANCE OR UNLAWFUL USE

Lessee agrees that they will not commit waste on the premises, or maintain or permit to be maintained a nuisance on the premises, or use or permit the premises to be used in an unlawful manner.

SECTION XIV - LESSEE'S HOLDING OVER

The parties agree that any holding over by lessee under this lease, without lessor's written consent, shall be a tenancy at will which may be terminated by lessor on 30 days' notice in writing.

SECTION XV - REDELIVERY OF PREMISES

At the end of the term of this lease, lessee shall quit and deliver up the premises to lessor in as good condition as they are now, ordinary wear, decay, and damage by the elements excepted.

SECTION XVI - DEFAULT

If lessee defaults in the payment of rent or any part of the rent at the times specified above, or if lessee defaults in the performance of or compliance with any other term or condition of this lease agreement *[or of the regulations attached to and made a part of this lease agreement, which regulations shall be subject to occasional amendment or addition by lessor]*, the lease, at the option of lessor, shall terminate and be forfeited, and lessor may reenter the premises and retake possession and recover damages, including costs and attorney fees. Lessee shall be given 30 days *[written]* notice of any default or breach. Termination and forfeiture of the lease shall not result if, within 15 days of receipt of such notice, lessee has corrected the default or breach or has taken action reasonably likely to effect correction within a reasonable time.

SECTION XVII - DESTRUCTION OF PREMISES AND EMINENT DOMAIN

In the event the leased premises are destroyed or rendered untenantable by fire, storm, or earthquake, or other casualty not caused by the negligence of lessee, or if the leased premises are taken by eminent domain, this lease shall be at an end from such time except for the purpose of enforcing rights that may have then accrued under this lease agreement. The rental shall then be accounted for between lessor and lessee up to the time of such injury or destruction or taking of the premises, lessee paying up to such date and lessor refunding the rent collected beyond such date. Should a part only of the leased premises be destroyed or rendered untenantable by fire, storm, earthquake, or other casualty not caused by the negligence of lessee, the rental shall abate in the proportion that the injured part bears to the whole leased premises. The part so injured shall be restored by lessor as speedily as practicable, after which the full rent shall recommence and the lease continue according to its terms. Any condemnation award concerning the leased premises shall belong exclusively to lessor.

SECTION XVIII - DELAY IN OR IMPOSSIBILITY OF DELIVERY OF POSSESSION

In the event possession cannot be delivered to lessee on commencement of the lease term, through no fault of lessor or lessor's agents, there shall be no liability on lessor or lessor's agents, but the rental provided in this lease agreement shall abate until possession is given. Lessor or lessor's agents shall have 30 days in which to give possession, and if possession is tendered within that time, lessee agrees to accept the leased premises and this lease agreement. In the event possession cannot be delivered within that time, through no fault of lessor or lessor's agents, then this lease and all rights under this lease agreement shall be at an end.

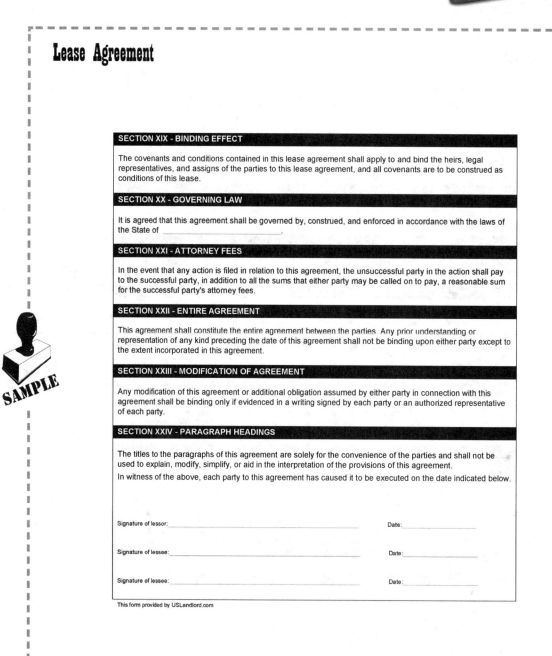

Lease Agreement

SECTION XIX - BINDING EFFECT

The covenants and conditions contained in this lease agreement shall apply to and bind the heirs, legal representatives, and assigns of the parties to this lease agreement, and all covenants are to be construed as conditions of this lease.

SECTION XX - GOVERNING LAW

It is agreed that this agreement shall be governed by, construed, and enforced in accordance with the laws of the State of _____.

SECTION XXI - ATTORNEY FEES

In the event that any action is filed in relation to this agreement, the unsuccessful party in the action shall pay to the successful party, in addition to all the sums that either party may be called on to pay, a reasonable sum for the successful party's attorney fees.

SECTION XXII - ENTIRE AGREEMENT

This agreement shall constitute the entire agreement between the parties. Any prior understanding or representation of any kind preceding the date of this agreement shall not be binding upon either party except to the extent incorporated in this agreement.

SECTION XXIII - MODIFICATION OF AGREEMENT

Any modification of this agreement or additional obligation assumed by either party in connection with this agreement shall be binding only if evidenced in a writing signed by each party or an authorized representative of each party.

SECTION XXIV - PARAGRAPH HEADINGS

The titles to the paragraphs of this agreement are solely for the convenience of the parties and shall not be used to explain, modify, simplify, or aid in the interpretation of the provisions of this agreement.

In witness of the above, each party to this agreement has caused it to be executed on the date indicated below.

Signature of lessor: _____   Date: _____

Signature of lessee: _____   Date: _____

Signature of lessee: _____   Date: _____

This form provided by USLandlord.com

Understanding Each Clause

Once again, **your lease agreement will vary from the clauses that have been broken down and explained below.** Nonetheless, **you should expect to see at least a few similarities** when compared against most rental agreements. The important point of this section is for you to *take the time to read and understand the basic principles.* Chances are, you may have never seen or even bothered to thoroughly read a lease agreement – so it will be well worth your effort to deal with a detailed analysis.

Subject of Lease

This section specifies the *physical location* (street address, city, county and state) **of the property that is the subject of the lease** and *spells out the purpose for which it will be used*. **If your lease does not specify an intended use, then you could (for example) use it for a business or exploit whatever zoning rights are available under the law. Therefore, most landlords will have the need to include a** *specified purpose* – so you don't operate a hair salon from their unit.

SECTION I - SUBJECT OF LEASE

Lessor shall lease to prospective lessee the residential property owned by prospective lessor located at
_____, _____, _____County,
_____, for lessee and their family to occupy and use as their residence.

Term of Lease

As you would expect, **you must define** *the term of the lease* and *options*. **Most leases are for one year**, but **you can always rent month-to-month** – *or even for several years,* if the landlord agrees. As far as the **right to renew, extend or modify**, *it's usually a good idea to push for the right to renew with a right of first refusal,* so no other tenant can occupy the unit at the end of your lease unless you decide to leave – this way, you'll have a place to live for another year or more, depending on your future needs.

SECTION II - TERM OF LEASE

The premises shall be leased to lessee for a period of _____ starting from _____. Any option to renew, extend or modify this lease shall require the approval of both the lessee and lessor.

Monthly Rental

Most lease agreements are paid monthly. This section spells out **how much the rent will be and when it is due.** The landlord **often collects the first month's rent in advance at the time of the lease signing** – *with all future payments due on a particular day of each month.* **This section is also where the landlord spells out the late fees and returned check fees.** *It's customary to charge a $50 late fee or 5% of the month's rent, if the tenant fails to pay by the fifth day* after the monthly due date. The **maximum late fees and returned check fees** that a landlord can charge **have been listed by state** in **Chapter 7.**

SECTION III - MONTHLY RENTAL

Lessee shall pay $ _____ per month as the monthly rental for the term of the lease with the first payment due on or before _____ , and subsequent payments on the ____ day of each succeeding month. This rental payment shall be subject to renegotiation by the parties at any time either of the parties exercises the option to renew the lease under the provisions of any subsequent lease agreement. It is agreed that if the rental payment is not received by the ____ day of the month, then a late fee of ____ shall be assessed and due immediately. Additional terms: _____

Security Deposit

This is an *essential* part of any lease executed today. A **security deposit** usually **protects against excessive wear and damage caused by the tenant,** *but can often include loss of rent.* **Some landlords also add a predetermined cleaning fee** (for example, $250) that is **automatically deducted upon moving out,** *regardless of whether or not there are any major problems.* Needless to say, **this entire clause can be negotiated** – including how much of a security deposit is required and what (if any) cleaning fee is to be charged. **Sometimes, a landlord will accept a security deposit to be paid in installments** (i.e., you'd pay $500 for the first three months instead of $1,500 upon moving in), so as to ease the burden on your cash reserves.

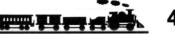

SECTION IV - SECURITY DEPOSIT

On the execution of this lease, lessee deposits with lessor $ _____ , receipt of which is acknowledged by lessor, as security for the faithful performance by lessee of the terms of this lease agreement, to be returned to lessee, without interest (unless required by law), on the full and faithful performance by lessee of the provisions of this residential lease agreement.

Number of Occupants

Most landlords will require a *limit on the number of occupants permitted for a rental* **and require** *additional occupants to be agreed to in writing.* **Common exceptions protecting you** under many housing laws are **pregnancy** and **adoption**. So, unless you become pregnant or adopt a child, **the only other way that you can** *legally* **add an additional occupant is with your landlord's written permission.**

SECTION V - NUMBER OF OCCUPANTS

Lessee agrees that the leased apartment shall be occupied by no more than ____ adults and ____ children under the age of 18 years without the prior, express, and written consent of lessor.

Assignment and Subletting

Most landlords will welcome the idea of you being able to **assign the lease or sublet the rental to someone else,** *so long as the landlord has the right to approve or reject the new party.* This is a useful clause if you are unsure about the length of your stay because of a new job opportunity on the horizon – or perhaps on account of the possibility of owning a home sooner than expected. To be fair, **the best you could expect is to have the landlord agree not to unreasonably withhold your request to assign or sublet.** *Your best bet would be to assign the lease so you are no longer responsible.* **Subletting traditionally holds the original tenant responsible if the new tenant fails to honor the lease.**

SECTION VI - ASSIGNMENT AND SUBLETTING

Without the prior, express, and written consent of lessor, lessee shall not assign this lease, or sublet the premises or any part of the premises. A consent by lessor to one assignment or subletting shall not be deemed to be a consent to any subsequent assignment or subletting.

Showing Property for Rental

When your lease is about to expire or terminate, this gives the landlord *the right to advertise the upcoming vacancy and show it to prospective tenants by giving you a reasonable advance notice*. As you could understand, **no landlord wants a vacant unit,** and **getting a head start (usually, 30 days) can only help to reduce the loss.** And the more accommodating you appear, the better your chances of reducing your loss regarding your security deposit. You wash the landlord's back and the landlord will wash yours. *While this is not an absolute, it is a reasonable clause for any landlord to require.* **The one thing worth modifying would be the amount of notice required and what time of day the unit may be shown.**

SECTION VII - SHOWING PROPERTY FOR RENTAL

Lessee grants permission to lessor to show the property to new rental applicants with reasonable advance notice and during reasonable hours of the day, within 30 days of the expiration of the term of this lease.

Entry for Inspection, Repairs and Alterations

Every landlord needs to have the right to enter his or her property with a reasonable amount of notice (*usually, 24-48 hours*) – and it is *customary to set up a window of time when you expect to remain at the property, not just a time when you will show up*. Not many landlords will use this clause to their advantage, because it's **not just for maintenance and repairs**; it's *also for inspecting the unit for potential lease violations*, such as unauthorized pets or occupants, hazardous materials… and the list goes on. A **list of each state's notice of entry requirements** has been provided in **Chapter 11.**

SECTION VIII - ENTRY FOR INSPECTION, REPAIRS AND ALTERATIONS

Lessor shall have the right to enter the leased premises with reasonable advance notice for inspection and whenever necessary to make repairs and alterations of the property.

Redecoration and Alterations

The last thing a landlord wants is for you to turn your outdoor patio into an indoor saloon. (Not that this may not be without its advantages…) But in all seriousness, **the idea behind this** *very important clause* **is to prevent outrageous occurrences such as these and to protect the sanctity of the rental from even the simple stuff like migraine-inducing wallpaper and/or paint colors.** Therefore, *it's reasonable for the landlord to require you to at least return the rental back to its original condition.* And **if you do intend on making any significant changes, it's best that you discuss this first with your landlord.** Minor modifications, such as ceiling fixtures that can be easily and safely removed and then *replaced* prior to vacating, are not a big deal.

SECTION IX - REDECORATION AND ALTERATIONS

It is agreed that lessee will not make or permit to be made any alterations, additions, improvements, or changes in the leased property without in each case first obtaining the written consent of lessor. A consent to a particular alteration, addition, improvement, or change shall not be deemed a consent to or a waiver of restrictions against alterations, additions, improvements, or changes for the future. All alterations, changes, and improvements built, constructed, or placed in the leased property by lessee, with the exception of fixtures removable without damage to the apartment and movable personal property, shall, unless otherwise provided by written agreement between lessor and lessee, be the property of lessor and remain in the leased apartment at the expiration or earlier termination of this lease.

Taxes and Utilities

Property taxes are always taken care of by the landlord and *personal taxes are – of course – the tenant's responsibility.* However, **utilities are** *always* **open to negotiation** – so **this section of the lease is an** *absolute "must-have,"* so that there is **no disagreement later as to who was supposed to have been paying for what.**

SECTION X - TAXES AND UTILITIES

A. Prospective lessor shall be liable for the payment of all real property taxes assessed against the residential premises as well as the following:

_____

B. Prospective lessee shall be liable for all personal property taxes as well as the following:

_____

Maintenance/Repairs

In commercial leases, the tenant is usually responsible for interior repairs and maintenance – but **in residential lease agreements,** *the landlord will usually take care of everything,* **unless you define each person's respective responsibilities for maintaining and repairing the unit**. Most of the time, **the landlord is responsible for anything that would render the unit uninhabitable** – like faulty appliances, plumbing, heating or air conditioning – but, ultimately, *you are entitled to draft your lease agreement any way you choose, as long as the law permits*.

SECTION XI - MAINTENANCE/REPAIRS

A. Prospective lessor shall be responsible for the following types of maintenance or repairs on the premises:

_____

B. Prospective lessee shall be responsible for the following types of maintenance or repairs on the premises:

_____

Animals

It's up to the landlord whether he or she wants to accept pets. According to the **American Pet Products Manufacturers Association (APPMA) 2005 – 2006 National Pet Owners Survey,** *39% of all U.S. households own at least one dog* and *34% own at least one cat*. After reading those statistics, **you could possibly be able to persuade your landlord to accept your pet.** Just be prepared to receive some resistance if you own a high-risk breed such as a cougar, pit bull, etc. **In the case of a resistant landlord, you may have to pony up some extra cash toward a non-refundable pet deposit.** However, if you just have a little Maltese or some similar breed, you may be able to negotiate a more favorable deposit (possibly even a refundable one). More on this topic and **pet agreements** can be found in **Chapter 6.**

SECTION XII - ANIMALS

Lessee shall keep no domestic or other animals in or about the property or on the property premises without the prior, express, and written consent of lessor.

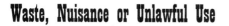

Waste, Nuisance or Unlawful Use

Simply put, **this has you agree not to collect extra mounds of nasty, smelly trash on the front lawn for your compost pile** or open up an auto restoration business with the backyard as the scrap yard/motor oil recycling center. If the rental happens to be in a **deed-restricted area**, then you will not be able to negotiate this clause. If there are no restrictions, then *be sure to discuss any specific needs you may have with the landlord.*

SECTION XIII - WASTE, NUISANCE OR UNLAWFUL USE

Lessee agrees that they will not commit waste on the premises, or maintain or permit to be maintained a nuisance on the premises, or use or permit the premises to be used in an unlawful manner.

Lessee's Holding Over

When the lease expires, there should be no holding over – *(you may not continue to stay)* – **unless you renew your lease annually or on a month-to-month basis.** This clause is added just in case you happen to stay without authorization. *It allows the landlord to give a 30-day notice to terminate your stay at any time.* If you do intend on renewing the lease, it is suggested that you give as much advance notice as possible.

SECTION XIV - LESSEE'S HOLDING OVER

The parties agree that any holding over by lessee under this lease, without lessor's written consent, shall be a tenancy at will which may be terminated by lessor on 30 days' notice in writing.

Redelivery of Premises

Very simply put, **this has you agree to give the property back in the same basic condition that it is was given to you** – *aside from minor wear and tear that is expected*. **If there is a specific part of the rental that you feel warrants special attention** – a part that's already in bad shape or prone to problems beyond your control – **this section is the place to note it.**

Default

This section spells out **what happens should you violate any term or condition of the lease agreement (past due rent, damage, nuisance, etc.).**   When a violation occurs, *usually the landlord will give the tenant an opportunity to correct whatever it may be or at least allow the tenant to show that he or she has initiated the appropriate steps to correct the problem*.

An unauthorized pet turns up on the premises. The landlord may then allow a reasonable amount of time for you to find the pet a new home. There is a great amount of flexibility in this section afforded to both parties when it comes to tolerance and time frames. Therefore, *this part should be modified according to your personal beliefs regarding how to reasonably handle lease violations*.

<u>NOTE</u>: **You must also take into account** *any requirements or provisions* **your** *local or state government* **may have regarding the landlord's right to terminate a lease agreement.**

SECTION XVI - DEFAULT

If lessee defaults in the payment of rent or any part of the rent at the times specified above, or if lessee defaults in the performance of or compliance with any other term or condition of this lease agreement *[or of the regulations attached to and made a part of this lease agreement, which regulations shall be subject to occasional amendment or addition by lessor]*, the lease, at the option of lessor, shall terminate and be forfeited, and lessor may reenter the premises and retake possession and recover damages, including costs and attorney fees. Lessee shall be given 30 days *[written]* notice of any default or breach. Termination and forfeiture of the lease shall not result if, within 15 days of receipt of such notice, lessee has corrected the default or breach or has taken action reasonably likely to effect correction within a reasonable time.

Destruction of Premises and Eminent Domain

Okay, you moved into your unit located in the Midwest – and, all of a sudden, a tornado wipes out the building while no one is there. This part of the lease explains that **if the property is essentially destroyed, the lease agreement terminates immediately –** *unless the unit is only partially damaged (and still habitable);* *then, you will pay* **only an agreed portion of the rent** *until the unit is fully restored*.

The outside porch blows away – you should have the rent reduced by the percentage of the porch that is no longer there. The other – albeit *extremely* rare – situation would be for the government to step in and take control of the property for some specified purpose (e.g., time of war, highway expansion plans, etc.), but, again, this is extremely rare.

EXAMPLE

SECTION XVII - DESTRUCTION OF PREMISES AND EMINENT DOMAIN

In the event the leased premises are destroyed or rendered untenantable by fire, storm, or earthquake, or other casualty not caused by the negligence of lessee, or if the leased premises are taken by eminent domain, this lease shall be at an end from such time except for the purpose of enforcing rights that may have then accrued under this lease agreement. The rental shall then be accounted for between lessor and lessee up to the time of such injury or destruction or taking of the premises, lessee paying up to such date and lessor refunding the rent collected beyond such date. Should a part only of the leased premises be destroyed or rendered untenantable by fire, storm, earthquake, or other casualty not caused by the negligence of lessee, the rental shall abate in the proportion that the injured part bears to the whole leased premises. The part so injured shall be restored by lessor as speedily as practicable, after which the full rent shall recommence and the lease continue according to its terms. Any condemnation award concerning the leased premises shall belong exclusively to lessor.

Delay in or Impossibility of Delivery of Possession

If, for some reason, **the property is *not* ready for you to move in on the effective date** of the lease agreement, **this clause allows the landlord a certain amount of time to get the property ready or the lease shall terminate**. So if the landlord is *in the process of making some repairs or improvements that may run behind schedule, you'll want to clearly define how much time you are willing to wait* (**if any at all**) *for the unit.*

SECTION XVIII - DELAY IN OR IMPOSSIBILITY OF DELIVERY OF POSSESSION

In the event possession cannot be delivered to lessee on commencement of the lease term, through no fault of lessor or lessor's agents, there shall be no liability on lessor or lessor's agents, but the rental provided in this lease agreement shall abate until possession is given. Lessor or lessor's agents shall have 30 days in which to give possession, and if possession is tendered within that time, lessee agrees to accept the leased premises and this lease agreement. In the event possession cannot be delivered within that time, through no fault of lessor or lessor's agents, then this lease and all rights under this lease agreement shall be at an end.

Binding Effect

This legal jargon basically says that **if you die, your estate is responsible for paying the remainder of the lease *or* if the lease is assigned to another person (upon approval of the landlord), all the terms and conditions of the lease agreement shall remain in full force**.

SECTION XIX - BINDING EFFECT

The covenants and conditions contained in this lease agreement shall apply to and bind the heirs, legal representatives, and assigns of the parties to this lease agreement, and all covenants are to be construed as conditions of this lease.

Governing Law

This aspect of the lease agreement stipulates the playing field in which any landlord-tenant legal entanglements are to be played out – which is, customarily, **the state in which the property is located.** *If you are coming from out of state, don't expect to be able to convince the landlord to agree to a different venue than where the property is located*. It is also common in this section to see a notation regarding **in which county** *any and all* **legal actions must be filed**.

SECTION XX - GOVERNING LAW

It is agreed that this agreement shall be governed by, construed, and enforced in accordance with the laws of the State of _____ .

Attorney Fees

This clause is **intended to deter you from filing frivolous lawsuits**. It simply states that **if a lawsuit is filed, the losing party must pay the winning party reasonable attorney fees –** *in addition to any monetary award ordered by the court*. This is another standard clause that won't be able to be negotiated because it is essentially fair to both sides.

SECTION XXI - ATTORNEY FEES

In the event that any action is filed in relation to this agreement, the unsuccessful party in the action shall pay to the successful party, in addition to all the sums that either party may be called on to pay, a reasonable sum for the successful party's attorney fees.

Entire Agreement

In case you have discussions with the landlord prior to – or even after – the execution of the lease that may be misconstrued by either party as a binding agreement, **this section clearly states that the only terms and conditions that are legally binding are the ones stated in the *written* lease agreement, *regardless* of what has been – *or will be* – said.**

SECTION XXII - ENTIRE AGREEMENT

This agreement shall constitute the entire agreement between the parties. Any prior understanding or representation of any kind preceding the date of this agreement shall not be binding upon either party except to the extent incorporated in this agreement.

Modification of Agreement

This section appropriately supports the **"Entire Agreement"** clause, by stating that *any and all* **changes to the lease must be *mutually agreed to in writing* by both the landlord and you, the tenant.**

SECTION XXIII - MODIFICATION OF AGREEMENT

Any modification of this agreement or additional obligation assumed by either party in connection with this agreement shall be binding only if evidenced in a writing signed by each party or an authorized representative of each party.

Paragraph Headings

We all have our own interpretation of agreements and *the simple statement contained within this clause* **eliminates at least one element from having to be debated and misinterpreted:** *all* **of the paragraph headings!**

SECTION XXIV - PARAGRAPH HEADINGS

The titles to the paragraphs of this agreement are solely for the convenience of the parties and shall not be used to explain, modify, simplify, or aid in the interpretation of the provisions of this agreement.

In witness of the above, each party to this agreement has caused it to be executed on the date indicated below.

Signature of lessor:_____   Date:_____

Signature of lessee:_____   Date:_____

Signature of lessee:_____   Date:_____

How to Negotiate Your List of Demands

Now that you've read an entire lease agreement, you've probably come up with several ideas regarding how you want to negotiate your lease. **The first thing you need to do is request a copy of the actual lease agreement used by your landlord, so you can have an opportunity to review it** (at least overnight). This way, you can go through each clause just as you did in this book to determine which ones you may have an issue with or simply need to clarify.

Life is giving and taking. **Don't expect to get everything you want, but you can sure try.** Nevertheless, *all lease negotiations generally follow the same process.* **The goal is to find a balance between your wants and needs, while being realistic about your chances at the same time.**

The Basic Steps to Negotiating a Lease:

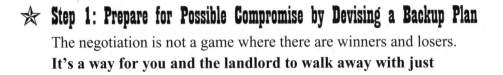

☆ Step 1: Prepare for Possible Compromise by Devising a Backup Plan

The negotiation is not a game where there are winners and losers. **It's a way for you and the landlord to walk away with just**

enough to keep you both happy. Therefore, you should devise a backup plan of alternatives to suggest – just in case.

 ## Step 2: Determine What You Can Give and What You Need in Return

Ask to review a copy of the lease agreement in advance to find out exactly what the landlord wants and what you are willing to accept. **Preliminary information is crucial to have before negotiating anything.**

Step 3: Start Out with Simple Requests

The landlord is much more willing to compromise if you **don't ask for too much in the beginning.**

Step 4: Empathize with the Landlord

Show that you understand the landlord's point of view; the landlord, in turn, will try to understand what you are saying as well. This will help you both come to an acceptable compromise.

Step 5: Keep Your Emotions in Check as the Negotiation Progresses

Remain calm as you negotiate and don't let your feelings get the best of you. **Remember, compromise does not equal failure.**

Step 6: Listen Very Carefully to the Landlord's Arguments

Zero in on any discrepancies as you negotiate; *the landlord may be bending the truth to his or her advantage.*

Step 7: Modify and Finalize the Lease Agreement in Writing

All final accommodations, exceptions, favors, gifts, or what have you, *must be written into the lease agreement.* Otherwise, your newly negotiated terms are not legally binding.

To assist you in determining which battles to choose, **a list of the most reasonable demands you may be entitled to have been summed up below.** You should **add or remove items from this list based upon specific clauses** contained in your landlord's lease agreement and your personal needs.

Reasonable Demands Worth Negotiating:

☆ Term of Lease

Whether it's month-to-month, semi-annual, annual or whatever, ***the length of your lease is worth discussing.***

☆ Monthly Rental

This is one of those things that is never set in stone, especially when dealing with individual landlords who own a house for rent. Apartment communities, on the other hand, may have a more difficult time with this, due to the potential backlash from other tenants if your rent is negotiated differently. However, **you may be able to negotiate some type of move-in incentive.**

☆ Security Deposit

Since you can usually expect to pay a security deposit, ***the best way to negotiate this aspect is to either ask for a reduction based upon your stellar creditworthiness or have it prorated over three months.*** Anything beyond that would be difficult for most landlords to accept.

☆ Assignment and Subletting

This becomes important if you are unsure of the length of your stay, because it provides a way out if you need to leave.

★ Redecoration and Alterations

If you intend on making any significant changes, this should be discussed and perhaps written into the lease agreement. **Especially** for those of you that would like to make serious modifications – such as putting in wood flooring, ceramic tile, etc. **This level or degree of change may even get you a credit toward a portion of your rent.**

★ Utilities

This applies more often to individual landlords. Once again, apartment communities will have policies that must be followed to ensure all tenants are treated equally. *Landlords (in today's rental market) will at least listen to what you have to propose and may surprise you by sometimes agreeing to it.*

★ Maintenance and Repairs

A maintenance-free lease on your part is of course best, but the details of your unit's requirements will have to be spelled out. Generally, **anything to keep the unit habitable that is subject to failure due to normal wear and tear should be the landlord's responsibility.**

★ Animals

This is another one of those negotiable factors. *Landlords can refuse to accept your dog, cat, python, fish tank, so you may have to throw a little extra their way to convince them that your little creature is landlord friendly.*

★ Cleaning Fee

If required by the landlord, *the importance of the cleaning fee is to ensure you will leave the unit neat, tidy and odor-free.* Therefore, if you can clean up after yourself and do a good job at

Everything U Need to Know...

polishing the rental, then you should ***ask for the cleaning fee to be listed as refundable or not subject to withholding, so long as you've cleaned the unit to a reasonable level of satisfaction.*** **Some state laws will automatically allow you one more opportunity to clean the unit before the landlord can deduct this fee from your security deposit.** ***States that specifically address cleaning fees*** are discussed in **Chapter 8.**

Moving In:
Why the First 24 Hours Is Critical

This Chapter Discusses:

★ **Capturing the Moment**
★ **Assessment of Condition**
★ **Addressing Issues**

And you thought all of the paperwork and legal mumbo jumbo was behind you because you just signed the lease and received your keys... Well, not quite yet. **You now have a limited amount of time to assess the rental property's condition before you accept the unit *"as-is."*** Kind of like inspecting a rental car before you drive it off the lot. **The last thing you need is to be held responsible for damage or other problems that occurred prior to your moving in** – and you'll most certainly want to make sure the unit is habitable before bothering to unload your U-Haul.

So, before you dump a single belonging into the middle of a room, follow the steps in this chapter to ensure your rights are protected. After all, you probably gave the landlord thousands of dollars upon signing the lease, so you deserve a unit that has been prepped and readied for your comfort.

Capturing the Moment

You don't need to make Spielberg or Lucas proud, but **you do need to document the condition of the property on some form of film medium** (e.g., **video tape, digital camera, Polaroid**). *Any* **item that appears to be excessively worn, damaged or inoperative should be filmed for your own protection – prior to unloading and unpacking your belongings.** This includes major appliances, wall and ceiling fixtures, heating and cooling units, hot water tanks, toilets, sinks, showers, flooring and yes, *even* the kitchen sink.

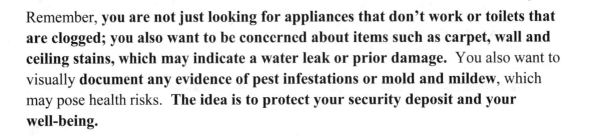

Remember, **you are not just looking for appliances that don't work or toilets that are clogged; you also want to be concerned about items such as carpet, wall and ceiling stains, which may indicate a water leak or prior damage.** You also want to visually **document any evidence of pest infestations or mold and mildew**, which may pose health risks. **The idea is to protect your security deposit and your well-being.**

Assessment of Condition

In addition to filming the unit for visual flaws all on your own, **the landlord should provide you with a checklist to make notations about the property's condition.** If not, **a sample checklist has been purposely provided in this section for your use,** because you need to take the rental for a test drive.

That's right – go ahead and flush all of the toilets, turn on the faucets, flick the switches, play with the appliances, kick on the thermostats and whatever else you can get your hands on – because **the visual recording of the previous section should be kept for your own use should there ever be a dispute.** But **the checklist,** on the other hand, **should be photocopied and given to your landlord to put him or her on notice of the condition of the property as it was observed the day you moved in.**

The **Assessment of Property Condition checklist** presented on the next seven pages is a **standard form that may be utilized as a template** if you desire to extract elements and create your own – or you may simply **print the form as it appears here from the enclosed CD-ROM.** Anything that doesn't apply may be easily crossed out.

Assessment of Condition

SAMPLE

Assessment of Condition of Rental Property

This checklist will help you protect your security deposit. Using the key on the right, fill in the letter that best describes the condition of your unit. This checklist must be returned within 3 days after the start of your lease. Before you move out, request a copy of this checklist, fill in the "End of Lease" column, and then return it so we may corroborate your assessment using the "Landlord's end-of-lease assessment" column.

Key	
Missing	M
Good condition	G
Scratched	S
Damaged	D
Broken	B
Repair needed	R

Exterior	Beginning of lease	End of lease	Landlord's end-of-lease assessment	Comments
Front door				
Front screen door				
Back door				
Back screen door				
Screens and storm windows				
Windows and frames				
Mailbox				
Doorbell				
Apartment number				
Garbage container				
Recycling containers				
Security intercom				
Other				

Page 1 of 7

Assessment of Condition

Kitchen	Beginning of lease	End of lease	Landlord's end-of-lease assessment	Comments
Windows				
Blinds/curtains				
Floor				
Walls				
Ceiling				
Lights and switches				
Outlets				
Stove				
Refrigerator				
Dishwasher				
Garbage disposal				
Sink				
Cabinets and counter				
Baseboards				
Trim				
Other				

Dining room	Beginning of lease	End of lease	Landlord's end-of-lease assessment	Comments
Windows				
Blinds/curtains				
Carpet or floor				
Walls				
Ceiling				
Lights and switches				
Outlets				
Baseboards				
Trim				
Other				

SAMPLE

SAMPLE

Assessment of Condition

Living room	Beginning of lease	End of lease	Landlord's end-of-lease assessment	Comments
Windows				
Blinds/curtains				
Carpet or floor				
Walls				
Ceilings				
Outlets				
Lights and switches				
Baseboards				
Trim				
Cable outlet				
Other				

Hallway and stairwell	Beginning of lease	End of lease	Landlord's end-of-lease assessment	Comments
Carpet or floor				
Walls				
Ceiling				
Lights and switches				
Outlets				
Baseboards				
Trim				
Stair treads				
Landing and handrail				
Other				

Assessment of Condition

Bedroom #1	Beginning of lease	End of lease	Landlord's end-of-lease assessment	Comments
Door				
Windows				
Blinds/curtains				
Carpet or floor				
Walls				
Ceiling				
Lights and switches				
Outlets				
Closet				
Baseboards				
Trim				
Other				

Bedroom #2	Beginning of lease	End of lease	Landlord's end-of-lease assessment	Comments
Door				
Windows				
Blinds/curtains				
Carpet or floor				
Walls				
Ceiling				
Lights and switches				
Outlets				
Closet				
Baseboards				
Trim				
Other				

SAMPLE

Assessment of Condition

SAMPLE

Bedroom #3	Beginning of lease	End of lease	Landlord's end-of-lease assessment	Comments
Door				
Windows				
Blinds/curtains				
Carpet or floor				
Walls				
Ceiling				
Lights and switches				
Outlets				
Closet				
Baseboards				
Trim				
Other				

Bathroom #1	Beginning of lease	End of lease	Landlord's end-of-lease assessment	Comments
Door				
Window				
Blinds/curtains				
Floor				
Walls				
Ceiling				
Sink				
Tub and/or shower				
Toilet				
Cabinet, shelves, closet				
Towel bars				
Lights and switches				
Outlets				
Baseboards				
Trim				
Other				

Assessment of Condition

Bathroom #2	Beginning of Lease	End of lease	Landlord's end-of-lease assessment	Comments
Door				
Window				
Blinds/curtains				
Floor				
Walls				
Ceiling				
Sink				
Tub and/or shower				
Toilet				
Cabinet, shelves, closet				
Towel bars				
Lights and switches				
Outlets				
Baseboards				
Trim				
Other				

Furniture	Beginning of Lease	End of Lease	Landlord's end-of-lease assessment	Comments
Kitchen chairs				
Tables				
End tables				
Lounge chairs				
Couches				
Lamps				
Desks				
Desk chairs				
Bookshelves				
Beds				
Mattresses				
Dressers				
Other				

Page 6 of 7

SAMPLE

Assessment of Condition

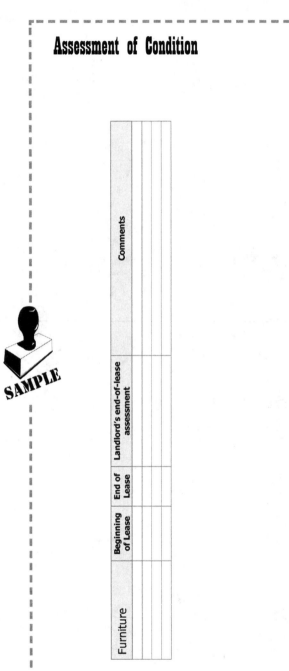

Furniture	Beginning of Lease	End of Lease	Landlord's end-of-lease assessment	Comments

Addressing Issues

After you've thoroughly inspected the unit, the next step before you're good to go is to **address any issues regarding problems with the unit.** *It's important before you proceed in taking anything up with the landlord to realistically determine whether or not it's a problem worth mentioning.* The reason for this is that **you want to choose your battles wisely, *because the last thing you want to do is present yourself as a problem tenant.*** Any issues (as stated in **Chapter 4**) brought to your landlord's attention **should be ones about legitimate safety concerns** or **ones that could affect your security deposit.**

Just remember – **you may need to ask your landlord for a favor one day, so you don't want to wear out your welcome.** This doesn't mean you should ever be afraid to speak up and stand up for your rights; just *ask yourself if this particular issue is really worth it.* Otherwise, **if it's a problem that can be easily resolved on your own without digging into your pockets or expending too much energy, you may want to go ahead and just take care of it.**

One story relevant to this point is shared from **AmerUSA.net** – where the tenants (husband and wife in their early 40s) once called a landlord (who lived three hours away from the rental) to request that he send out a pest control service to remove a single golf-ball-size wasp nest that appeared under the outside porch. Now, it's a given that no one wants to get stung by a wasp, but that's why they sell over-the-counter spray available in every grocery store for a few dollars. **Unless it's a major infestation, ordinary occurrences such as these should not involve your landlord.**

For those problems that do need the landlord's attention, **it is suggested that you make a personal appearance or phone call and approach the matter in a casual, but sincere, manner with your checklist in hand.** *Your first approach should always be friendly and conversational.* **There is no need to make any serious demands until you see that the landlord fails to respond to your concerns in a satisfactory manner.**

If you encounter some resistance (although, it's rare at such an early stage), **don't get into a heated argument – simply dismiss yourself and tell the landlord you will give it some more thought.** Then **go back home and prepare a letter that itemizes your concerns** and **be sure to state why you believe the landlord would be responsible to take care of them.** In closing, **you should indicate that you do not believe your concerns are unreasonable and wish for a quick resolution.** *The tone of this letter should be one of concern,* **but a little relaxed** (not too formal).

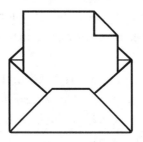

If you continue to receive resistance, then a second (final) letter needs to be formatted and written in a more serious legal tone – *because you will be offering the landlord an ultimatum.* Needless to say, at this point, **the relationship with your landlord will definitely go sour and may require a small claims court to intervene if tenancy is terminated and either party owes the other money.**

This is certainly not the way you want to begin, but **the second (final) letter needs to instruct the landlord that if the problems with the rental are not resolved by a particular date, you will have no choice but to terminate your tenancy and request your security deposit and any unused portion of your rent to be returned.** *If the unit was completely uninhabitable* (very rare, as this would violate most local and state laws)*, you would be entitled to receive all of your money back.*

Chapter 6

Pets and Other Animals:
How to Rent with Your Little/Big Roommates

This Chapter Discusses:

★ **Fish Tanks**

★ **Cats**

★ **Dogs**

★ **Exotic Animals**

★ **Pet Agreements and Deposits**

★ **Pet Owner Responsibilities**

As mentioned in **Chapter 3**, it's **usually in the landlord's best interest to accept pets** (at least dogs and cats), **because over a third of all households have one. A landlord would have a better chance of filling his or her vacancy if it's marketed to a larger audience than restricting the prospects to ones without pets.** Ironically, the landlord's reason for rejecting pets usually isn't the increased liability or threat posed to fellow neighbors; it's the threat posed to the baseboards, carpeting, doors and furnishings that weighs heavy on his or her mind.

Of course, there are landlords concerned about the safety of other inhabitants, neighbors and the community at large when you tell them that your two pitbulls would like to move in with you. **This chapter will discuss common landlord concerns and requirements, as well as your rights and responsibilities as a tenant with a pet.**

Fish Tanks

This is an especially interesting topic because it's often equated to the whole issue with waterbeds from the 1980s. As a whole, **with any apparatus designed to hold dozens or hundreds of gallons of water in a rental unit (or home), landlords and insurance companies get nervous.** *Water is bad news; one mishap could spell disaster.*

This is why landlords who *are* willing to accept fish tanks **sometimes require deposits** or for you to agree to a **specific placement of the tank.** In other words, the fish tank must be positioned in the kitchen or on some tiled surface. Small fish bowls and aquariums are seldom ever discussed or disclosed. However, larger freshwater or saltwater displays *can pose a problem for some landlords.*

Fortunately, unless the landlord specifically asks, **you are not required to disclose you even plan on rooming with some marine life.** However, if the topic does come up and there is a little resistance, *be prepared to reassure the landlord and possibly offer a refundable deposit that must be returned to you upon vacating* – as long as the fish tank never causes any damage. In all reality, fish tank mishaps are seldom encountered, but **when they do happen, it's a big mess** – even when it's only just a few gallons.

Cats

Most landlords generally don't have a problem with cats, although there are a few out there that will only accept **cats that have been declawed** – especially those landlords that offer furnished units, in which case the deposit needed to offset the potential for damage would be too great for most tenants to be able to handle.

According to the **Humane Society, declawing cats is a matter of continuing controversy and should only be considered as a last resort because of the potential complications for the cat because it's more than a manicure** – *it's a surgical procedure that traditionally involves the amputation of the last bone of each toe.* The **Humane Society** advocates that *properly educated owners can easily train their cats* to use their claws in a manner that allows a peaceful existence. **Declawing should be reserved** *only* **for those rare cases in which a cat has a medical problem** that would warrant such surgical procedure or, after exhausting all other options, it becomes clear that the cat cannot be properly trained – and, as a result, would jeopardize your tenancy.

If faced with this issue concerning your cat, *consult your veterinarian on your options and don't ever let the landlord sway your decision* – **this is something for you and your veterinarian to decide.** Just be prepared to walk away and find a landlord who accepts your cat "as-is."

Dogs

There is an ongoing debate about the increased risk to humans by certain dog breeds. Some say it's how they are raised and nurtured, while others say it's genetically controlled behavior. Regardless of what your beliefs are, **there are quite a few landlords and insurance companies that have labeled some dog breeds to be high-risk or dangerous – based upon reports from the American Veterinary Medical Association, the Center for Disease Control and the Humane Society.** The fact of the matter is *you won't be able to win a debate against a landlord or insurance company that has adopted a strict no pet (or no breed) policy.* Human fatalities and bodily harm aside, **there still remains the issue of pet stains, odor and damage** that landlords are usually concerned about.

The best thing to offer a landlord (aside from cash) is **a stellar recommendation from a current or previous landlord concerning your pet and the condition of the premises.** *Landlords need to feel comfortable about whom they are renting to, including the entire household that accompanies the tenant.* Whether it's corporate-controlled complexes or individually owned properties, **all landlords have a large investment at stake** – and, for some, it may even be their only source of income.

There have been **thousands of stories about thousands of dollars in property damage caused by pets and their neglectful owners** (see the **final section of this chapter**, regarding **your responsibilities**). So, it's important to understand the reasons behind any resistance you may encounter – in order to present your best rebuttal. Of course, **if you have a disability and your animal companion is a designated service animal, no landlord can turn you down – thanks to the** *Americans with Disabilities Act.*

Exotic Animals

So you don't care for cats and dogs. Instead, you have a fondness for 16-foot pythons or little monkeys. **Since landlords will most likely not have an exotic pet policy or guidelines, their questions may only pertain to cats and dogs.** If that is the case, then *you are not obligated to disclose your hairy tarantula collection that you love to allow to roam free.* However, **if the landlord has a blanket questionnaire about pets and any other animals, you** *must* **answer it truthfully to avoid any future claims of lease violations.**

There is certainly nothing wrong with the many unorthodox pets that are quiet and easy to manage. The problem is when **you own an obnoxiously loud squawking bird** from some tropical paradise. It may be pretty to look at for some, but *the vast majority of people would soon be annoyed* at the break of dawn or the onset of dusk, when the squawk box goes off and on, off and on, off and on... **In this instance, it may be unreasonable to expect to find a suitable place to live in a community building.** Instead, *you may want to find a house that doesn't share walls with your neighbors.* Just don't keep your feathered friend on the back porch for the neighborhood to hear.

By the way, **some exotic animals either are outlawed or must be licensed in certain jurisdictions.** Obviously, *it's your responsibility to make sure your cool little creature has been properly permitted.* Otherwise, **you may be forced to make a decision – either move or get rid of your exotic pet.** Yes, **it's your right to own any legally permissible pet,** *but your landlord also has the right to refuse you tenancy* – so **choose wisely when shopping for a pet,** especially when you plan to rent for a few more years.

Pet Agreements and Deposits

As mentioned in **Chapter 3, landlords will often charge an additional deposit if you intend on boarding a pet.** The deposit is *usually accompanied by a separate agreement that is added as an addendum to the lease agreement.* In order to simplify matters, **landlords will commonly state that the pet deposit is non-refundable.** This *alleviates the possibility of having you dispute the occurrence of any pet odor, stains, flea infestations or damage* – and also considers the fact that pet mishaps happen rather frequently. **However, when the rental market is in a slump,** *there is no reason why the pet deposit can't be negotiated to be refundable.* But don't be surprised if the landlord then **requires you to have the carpet professionally cleaned and treated** for fleas, as a matter of precaution.

A **copy of a pet agreement appears on the next two pages** for you to see some of the common requirements. One of the **more notable aspects of such an agreement addresses the issue of breeding and what must be done if more animals are born on the premises.** Just be sure **if you *are* in the puppy business, that you are properly licensed to conduct business wherever you are located** – and that **your lease agreement doesn't preclude you from operating such a home business.**

Note: Service animals for those with disabilities are *exempt from pet agreements and deposit fees.*

Pet Agreement

Instructions:
1. Insert your IMAGE or LOGO (optional)
2. Complete PET AGREEMENT FIELDS
3. REPLACE ALL of this text with YOUR contact info
4. Click on 'PRINT FORM' when finished

Everything U Need to Know...

Click here to insert image/logo

Pet Agreement

AMENDMENT TO LEASE

For valuable consideration, receipt of which is hereby acknowledged, _____, "Lessor" and _____, "Lessee", parties to the Lease Agreement made for property located at _____, _____, _____ County, _____ and dated on _____ agree to modify and amend said Lease Agreement in the following way(s):

Lessee desires to keep the following described pet in the dwelling referred to above:

Type: _____

Breed: _____

Weight: _____

TERMS AND CONDITIONS

1. Lessee agrees that they are solely responsible for the maintenance of the above described pet, and agree to keep their pet under control at all times.

2. Lessee agrees to keep their pet restrained, but not tethered, when it is outside their dwelling.

3. Lessee agrees to adhere to local ordinances, including leash and licensing requirements.

4. Lessee agrees not to leave their pet unattended for unreasonable periods.

5. Lessee agrees to clean up after their pet and to dispose of their pet's waste properly and quickly.

6. Lessee agrees not to leave food or water for their pet or any other animal outside their dwelling where it may attract other animals.

7. Lessee agrees to keep their pet from being unnecessarily noisy or aggressive and causing any annoyance or discomfort to others and will remedy immediately any complaints made.

8. Lessee agrees to provide their pet with an identification tag while on the premises.

9. Lessee agrees not to breed or allow the pet to reproduce. If this should occur, the pet's offspring must be placed within 10 weeks of birth.

10. Lessee agrees to immediately pay for any damage, loss, or expense caused by their pet, and in addition, they will add $ _____ to their security/cleaning deposit, which may be used for cleaning, repairs or delinquent rent when Lessee vacates. This added deposit, or what remains of it when pet damages have been assessed, will be returned to Lessee within 10 days after they have proved that they no longer keep this pet.

11. Lessee agrees that this Agreement applies only to the specific pet described above.

12. Lessee agrees that the Lessor reserves the right to revoke permission to keep the pet should the Lessee break this agreement. Lessee will be given 10 days to remove the pet from the premises.

Pet Agreement

TERMS AND CONDITIONS (Continued)

13. Any animals on the property not registered under this agreement will be presumed to be strays and will be removed according to law, at the option of the Lessor.

ORIGINAL LEASE AGREEMENT

All other terms and covenants of the original Lease Agreement shall remain in full force and effect.

In witness of the above, each party to this agreement has caused it to be executed on the date below.

Signature of lessor: _____ Date: _____

Signature of lessee: _____ Date: _____

Signature of lessee: _____ Date: _____

This form provided by USLandlord.com

Pet Owner Responsibilities

For most of you who are responsible adults and great pet parents, this is a given. But don't be surprised – *there are many tenants who not only neglect their pets, but disrespect their rental and those of their neighbors* – which has only compounded many landlords' paranoia.

Unless your pet is properly trained, you may want to consider crating or caging it while you are away. *Most of the damage occurs when the tenant is not home, so use your best judgment.* **If you are going to be gone all day, your pet may not be able to prevent itself from urinating all over the place.** A sensible alternative may be to **hire a pet walker** or **buy a crate** to control and isolate any possible damage.

As if you didn't already know most of the information contained within, **here is a list of the most common pet owner responsibilities for those that intend on renting...**

☆ Common Pet Owner Responsibilities:

♦ **Provide good nutrition, grooming, exercise, flea control, routine veterinary care and yearly inoculations.** *Dogs and cats must wear identification tags and collars* **whenever** *outside the unit.*

♦ **Clean up after your pet inside the rental unit and anywhere on the development property.** A "pooper scooper" and disposable plastic bags should be used. **Pet debris should not be deposited in a toilet.** *You will most likely be responsible for any blockages that occur.*

♦ **Pet blankets and bedding should not be cleaned or washed in a communal laundry room** *for hygienic reasons.*

♦ **The outside patio, porch or deck** – if any – **should be kept clean and free of pet odors, insect infestation, waste and litter** *at all times.*

♦ You must **restrain and prevent the pet from gnawing, chewing, scratching or otherwise defacing the doors, walls, windows and floor covering of your unit, other units and common areas** – *as well as all shrubs and landscaping.*

♦ **Pets should not be tied up outside or left unattended on a patio, porch or deck** *at any time.*

♦ **Do not alter your unit, patio, deck, or other outside area to create an enclosure for an animal** *without the expressed written permission of the landlord.*

♦ **Pets should be restrained at all times when outside.** *No pet should be loose in hallways, elevators or other common areas.*

♦ **Any visitors you have with pets** should generally **conform to the landlord's policy.**

♦ **Pets should not be allowed to disturb the health, safety, rights, comfort or quiet enjoyment of your neighbors.** *Excessive barking, whining, chirping – or other unruly behavior – needs to be controlled.*

Chapter 7

The Monthly Rent:
Paid as Agreed

This Chapter Discusses:

★ **Making the Payment**

★ **Being Late**

★ **Bouncing Your Rent Check**

★ **Rent Increases**

★ **Rent Control**

Aside from having to abide by the other stipulations in a lease agreement, **this is the most important one with which you need to concern yourself, as far as protecting your right to continue to occupy the rental unit.** Most landlords can tolerate lease agreement infractions to a degree except for this one – *this is the lifeline between you and your landlord.* **As long as you continue to feed it every month with your money, your landlord-tenant relationship should work out just fine (most of the time).** However, if you fail to keep the cash coming once a month, you'll jeopardize your right to tenancy. Therefore, **this chapter will review the basic aspects of your monthly rent, including your landlord's obligations and your rights and responsibilities.**

Making the Payment

Will that be cash, check or charge? Actually, *that should be check.* **It's the easiest and best way to document that your rent has been paid.** *Paying by cash is not a wise thing to do* – even if you're able to get a receipt from the landlord, **there's no better document than a canceled check** that's been processed through the Federal Reserve System. **Receipts may be subject to verification of authenticity.** *A canceled check, on the other hand, is seldom questioned.*

Now, if you don't have a checking account, **the second best thing is to pay by certified funds** – such as a **money order** or **cashier's check,** depending on the amount of your rent. **Money order limits** are typically $1,000 per money order and are sold for just a few dollars, regardless of the amount. A **cashier's check** has **no limit imposed on the amount** of the check – however, it is sold for $5. Although, **as long as you have a relationship with a bank, that fee may be waived.** *If not, find a friendlier bank.*

The only difference in using certified funds instead of a personal check is **the tremendous inconvenience involved to confirm if a money order or cashier's check was cashed.** *Banks are not the easiest to deal with when it comes to retrieving a document.* On the other hand, **personal checks that have been canceled** are often viewable with the help of the latest online banking systems. If not, then copies are mailed to you along with your monthly checking account statement.

The important point of this section is to have some means of documenting that your payment was made! Unfortunately, *unless you do get some sort of receipt issued by either the landlord or postal carrier showing that your check was delivered, the landlord could still claim he or she never received the payment at all or it was late.* This rarely happens – but if it ever does, **you should seriously consider sending your future payments using some type of delivery confirmation service**… especially if you suspect the landlord of any wrong doing (i.e., purposely delaying the receipt of payments to charge a late fee). *Once again, these types of circumstances are very rare and sending it by mail (or even dropping it off) is* *sufficient without asking for a receipt.* Just use the "first time" rule. Once a problem such as this happens for the first time, *then* switch to a more official delivery method. Just be sure you *don't live by the "first time" rule when using cash* – that could prove to be a very expensive mistake, even happening for the first time.

Being Late

First of all, before discussing the legalities of being late and the laws for each state about penalties and so forth, **it's always best to contact the landlord with as much advance notice as possible to notify him or her that you intend on being late for the upcoming month's payment.** As long as your delinquency doesn't occur with any regularity, paying your rent on time is your best bet for keeping your relationship with your landlord in good shape. **Most landlords have their own obligations** (i.e., their own mortgage payments and bills) **and so they would appreciate some early warning to be better able to cope with their own personal finances.** Chances are, **they've been in your situation before and just want to be respected** (*not disrespected* by your failing to pay rent on time without any type of prior communication).

So what rights do you have to be late? Well, actually – none. *Unless the property becomes completely uninhabitable, you are still responsible for paying your rent.* In some instances, if only a portion of the property is damaged, but the property as a whole is still inhabitable, then your lease agreement or your state may allow for rent to be prorated. **Prorating involves only paying a portion of the rent based on how much space of your unit is in disrepair.** However, instead of trying to perform some ridiculous calculation to determine what percentage of the unit is technically out of service, **landlords will often work with you on coming to a reasonable agreement.**

By the way, **if there is ever an issue where you are not completely satisfied with your tenancy,** *don't ever hold back on your rent payment as a matter of protest* **unless the property is uninhabitable.** Otherwise (while you may feel you have every right to not pay your rent), **you could be wrong in the eyes of the law and risk**

breaching your lease agreement – which would only give your landlord better ammunition to use in terminating your tenancy.

If you're late for the sake of being late (i.e., you just don't have the money to pay your rent on time), then **depending on your state, your landlord may impose a penalty, which must be paid in addition** to your regularly scheduled rent. **A chart is provided on the next three pages, which summarizes the permissible late fee amounts for each state.** *Notice some states require the late fee to be written into the lease agreement* (this same rule, as you'll learn throughout the rest of this book, *also applies* to many other fees and penalties that a landlord wishes could be charged).

Late Fees

Alabama	No statute
Alaska	No statute
Arizona	Late fees must be reasonable and indicated in the lease agreement.
Arkansas	No statute
California	Late fees must be close to the landlord's actual losses and indicated in the lease agreement as follows: "Because landlord and tenant agree that actual damages for late rent payments are very difficult or impossible to determine, landlord and tenant agree to the following stated late charge as liquidated damages."
Colorado	No statute
Connecticut	Late fees can be charged when rent is 9 days late.
Delaware	Late fees cannot be more than 5% of the rent amount due and can be charged when the rent is more than 5 days late. If the landlord does not have an office within the rental property's county, the tenant has an additional 3 days before late fees can be charged.
District of Columbia	No statute
Florida	No statute
Georgia	No statute
Hawaii	No statute
Idaho	No statute
Illinois	No statute
Indiana	No statute
Iowa	Late fees cannot be more than $10 a day with a maximum of $40 a month allowed.
Kansas	No statute
Kentucky	No statute
Louisiana	No statute
Maine	Late fees cannot be more than 4% of the rent amount due for a 30-day period and must be indicated in writing to the tenant at the start of their tenancy. Late fees can be charged when rent is 15 days late.
Maryland	Late fees cannot be more than 5% of the rent amount due.

Massachusetts	Late fees can be charged when rent is 30 days late.
Michigan	No statute
Minnesota	No statute
Mississippi	No statute
Missouri	No staute
Montana	No statute
Nebraska	No statute
Nevada	Late fees must be indicated in the lease agreement.
New Hampshire	No statute
New Jersey	Late fees can be charged when rent is 5 days late.
New Mexico	Late fees cannot be more than 10% of the rent amount due per rental period. Tenant must be notified of the late fee charged by the end of the next rental period.
New York	No statute
North Carolina	Late fees cannot be more than 5% of the rent amount due or $15, whichever is greater, and can be charged when rent is 5 days late.
North Dakota	No statute
Ohio	No statute
Oklahoma	No statute
Oregon	Late fees cannot be more than a reasonable amount charged by others in the same market if a flat fee is utilized; if a daily charge is utilized, it cannot be more than 6% of the reasonable flat fee with a maximum of 5% of the rent amount due per rental period allowed. Late fees can be charged when rent is 4 days late and must be indicated in the lease agreement.
Pennsylvania	No statute
Rhode Island	No statute
South Carolina	No statute
South Dakota	No statute
Tennessee	Late fees can be charged when rent is 5 days late and cannot be more than 10% of the late rent amount. However, if the fifth day is a weekend or holiday and the tenant pays the rent amount due on the following business day, a late fee cannot be charged.

Texas	Late fees must be reasonable and close to the landlord's actual losses. Late fees must be indicted in the lease agreement and can be charged when the rent is 2 days late. Late fees can include an initial fee as well as a daily fee for each day the rent is late thereafter.
Utah	No statute
Vermont	No statute
Virginia	No statute
Washington	No statute
West Virginia	No statute
Wisconsin	No statute
Wyoming	No statute

Bouncing Your Rent Check

Just when you thought one fee was enough, here comes another. There's little in life that's as humiliating as bouncing a check when it's intended for someone important, such as your landlord. Once again, **if you happen to catch word of your bank returning a check unpaid, it would be a good idea to alert your landlord and make arrangements to replace the check with a more reliable payment method** (e.g., money order or cashier's check). ***Don't wait for your landlord to find out the hard way.*** It's a good idea to admit your error right away. As mentioned, **it's this type of open relationship that really works in your favor when help is truly needed** – and **now** would be that time, because your landlord could charge you a late fee on top of a bounced check fee, if your full and final payment isn't received on time and ultimately honored.

However, **if you catch wind of the returned check and notify the landlord before he or she finds out** – or, better yet, you notify the landlord and make good on your rent payment immediately – **he or she probably won't even charge you a late fee, just a returned check fee.**

Returned (bounced) check fees vary from state to state. So, **to better assist you in understanding what a landlord can charge you if your check is returned unpaid, a chart is provided on the next two pages showing exactly what each state allows.**

Returned Check Fees

Alabama	$30 - Check writer is also responsible for all other costs of collection.
Alaska	$30
Arizona	$25
Arkansas	$25
California	$25
Colorado	$20 - Check writer is also responsible for all other costs of collection.
Connecticut	$20 - Check writer is also responsible for all other costs of collection.
Delaware	$40
District of Columbia	$25
Florida	Checks from (1) $0.01-$50.00 = $25.00 fee, (2) $50.01-$300.00 = $30.00 fee, (3) $300.01 and over = the greater of $40.00 fee or 5% of the face amount of the check. Check writer is also responsible for all other costs of Collection.
Georgia	$30 or 5% of the face amount of the check, whichever is greater.
Hawaii	$30 - Check writer is also responsible for all other costs of collection.
Idaho	$20 - Check writer is also responsible for all other costs of collection.
Illinois	$25 - Check writer is also responsible for all other costs of collection.
Indiana	$20 - Check writer is also responsible for all other costs of collection.
Iowa	$30
Kansas	$30
Kentucky	$25
Louisiana	$25 or 5% of the face amount of the check, whichever is greater.
Maine	$25
Maryland	$35
Massachusetts	$25
Michigan	$25
Minnesota	$30 - Check writer is also responsible for all other costs of collection and civil penalties may be imposed for nonpayment.

Mississippi	$40
Missouri	$25
Montana	$30
Nebraska	$35
Nevada	$25
New Hampshire	$25
New Jersey	$30
New Mexico	$30
New York	$20 - Check writer is also responsible for all other costs of collection.
North Carolina	$25
North Dakota	$30
Ohio	$30 or 10% of the face amount of the check, whichever is greater.
Oklahoma	$25
Oregon	$25
Pennsylvania	$30
Rhode Island	$25
South Carolina	$30
South Dakota	$40
Tennessee	$30 - Check writer is also responsible for all other costs of collection.
Texas	$30 - Other costs of collection may be charged.
Utah	$20 - Check writer is also responsible for all other costs of collection.
Vermont	$25
Virginia	$35
Washington	$30 - This amount is assessed as a Handling Fee for returned checks. Check writer is also responsible for all other costs of collection.
West Virginia	$25
Wisconsin	$20 - Check writer is also responsible for all other costs of collection.
Wyoming	$25 - Check writer is also responsible for all other costs of collection.

Rent Increases

Every year, the cost of living index goes up – so why not your rent? Well, *it sometimes will upon the renewing of your lease.* Annual lease agreements are seldom written with rent increases built in – so once you enter into a lease, you're protected for 12 months or whatever the term may be. *The problem comes when you try to renew.*

Landlords (in most instances) have the right to charge a modest increase each year. *But whether or not the rental market will be able to bear such an increase is another issue.* As with anything else, **rental amounts are based upon the basic law of supply and demand,** as seen on everyday retail store shelves. So unless there is a significant demand for places to rent because the vacancies are low, you'll probably be able to renew without being charged more.

This topic brings up **an important point about negotiating lease agreements:** *Never agree to any rent increase that may occur during the term of your lease.* **This is best left to be negotiated at the end of your lease** if you've been given the option to renew. *Even better* **would be to stipulate that you have the right to renew the lease at the same amount of rent** – *so an increase from the landlord isn't even possible.*

Unless your local government offers a rent adjustment program, you live in a rent control area (as discussed in the next section) or you reside under the protection of the Department of Housing and Urban Development's (HUD) Section 8 housing assistance program, **landlords can increase your rent to whatever they choose.** However, unless they are just not happy with your tenancy, *they seldom try to push the rent up to an extraordinary amount.* The basic logic applies: **If it's not broken, don't fix it! Landlords will usually welcome a tenant back and for the same amount of rent.** *Many landlords have never implemented an increase for five or more years for the same tenant.*

Since rent increases are regulated by local governments, *you should contact your city or county housing department to inquire about any municipal codes or laws that may be in effect to protect you.* Although you'd think that landlords would be aware of what they can or can't do, **there are quite a few out there that are ignorant when it comes to the rules and regulations.**

Rent Control

Rent control refers to laws or ordinances that control the renting of residential housing by imposing some form of ceiling or limit to the amount for which a residential property can be rented. *Few cities in the United States have rent control laws in place.* Among the more notable ones are San Francisco, Washington, DC and New York City. However, **there are smaller communities that also have rent control** in California – notably, Santa Monica, Berkeley and West Hollywood, along with many small towns in New Jersey, such as Camden. Up until recently, cities such as Boston and Cambridge, Massachusetts used to have rent control laws, but those were revoked – although there are current attempts in Massachusetts to try and resurrect the local government's ability to control rent.

The purpose behind the concept of **rent control is to prevent landlords from imposing increases that force key workers or vulnerable people to leave an area.** *Maintaining a supply of affordable housing is essential to sustaining an economy.* Homeowners who support rent control point to community instability caused by high or frequent rent increases – and the effect on schools and organizations when tenants move more frequently. However, some claim that rent control is bad for the economy, because landlords are restricted in how much rent they may charge – and so they are less willing to acquire more housing in the area. Since supply is then perpetually low, landlords also don't have to worry about many tenants leaving, so they can purposely defer maintenance, in order to afford to absorb the lower rental income.

For the most part, **rent control is being slowly eliminated** – but *if you are unsure about the laws of your local area, contact your city or county government to see if some form of rent control or stabilization is in effect to protect you.*

Moving Out:
What to Do Before It's Time to Say Goodbye

This Chapter Discusses:

★ **Notifying Your Landlord**
★ **Cleaning Up After Yourself**
★ **Reassessing the Property's Condition**

You obviously don't need to be told how to coordinate the removal of your belongings and the termination or transfer of your utility accounts (e.g., cable, electric, gas, phone and water). The purpose of this chapter is to **make sure you're aware of exactly how to protect your legal rights before you pack up and hit the road.** If you leave without tying up any loose ends, *you could be subject to fines, penalties and even a bad reference* from your (now) previous landlord.

Notifying Your Landlord

Rarely are you ever required to notify a lender that you intend to move – this would only be found in lease agreements that have *automatic renewal clauses* should you fail to notify the landlord of your intention to vacate. Usually, **the landlord will be sending you a notice reminding you that your lease will be expiring soon with further instructions regarding renewing it**, etc. However, *as a courtesy and to comply with those few cities and states that require notice to be given, it's always best to give as much advance notice as possible (at least 30 days, but preferably 60 days).* **Maintaining your relationship with your landlord is especially vital toward the end** because (1) **you never know if you'll need your landlord as a reference** and (2) **you want every penny of your security deposit returned to you.**

Landlords appreciate being notified at least 30 days in advance – so they can begin to advertise the upcoming vacancy. At this point, **it's also a nice gesture on your part to practically encourage your landlord to show the unit during the last month of your stay.** Obviously, *these showings should be scheduled in advance and occur during reasonable hours* – but **offering this opportunity** (even when it's not written into your lease agreement) **just adds a little extra seasoning to the "goodwill" flavor**, with hopes that the landlord will reciprocate.

When it comes time to notify your landlord of your intention to move, **a phone call or a face-to-face conversation will usually be sufficient** – unless you deem it necessary to follow it up with a **friendly letter.** *Don't use this time to vent about any current or previous issues you may have had with the landlord, neighbors or the unit.* **Only** after you've finally moved on and into another place to live should you even *consider* expressing your opinion. This may appear to go against the grain of your beliefs, but *part of the landlord-tenant relationship includes the subtle use of manipulation.* Unless you're seeking an immediate change to the events at hand, **there is no point to ruffle any feathers until you are free and clear.**

By the way, *the same advice is given to landlords as well.* **They, too, should not in** *any* **way be confrontational with a tenant** – if for no other reason than to preserve the condition of the unit from suddenly overflowing toilets and sinks from clogged drains or loose gaskets.

Cleaning Up After Yourself

Your mother told you the importance of this a million times and you probably never thought it would ever ring true (financially, at least). But *when it comes to rental property, you need to treat the final days of your stay as if you were a guest in someone else's home.* **Nothing more should be expected of you than to leave the property in the same condition as it was when you arrived.** This is **why your initial assessment should have been completely and thoroughly documented,** as mentioned in **Chapter 5.**

Cleaning up after yourself applies to more than just a little spit and Windex. *It refers to returning the unit to its original shape.* Any fixtures, appliances or wall treatments that were your own idea **need to be removed or changed back**, *unless* you have been given an okay by your landlord to leave certain items "as-is." However, *if this is the case, you need to have the landlord sign off on each of these items.* The best way to approach this is to **prepare a list for the landlord and have him or her sign stating that each altered item is okay to be left in its current state.** Granted, handshakes are sometimes good enough – but any attorney will tell you to *get it in writing.*

For those items and changes that are not okay with your landlord, be sure you correct them in order to avoid being charged cleaning and restoration fees that (with today's prices) **could** *easily* **exceed your security deposit.** *Having your landlord sue you for additional expenses would cause even a bigger problem and headache than having to fix a few things, strip some wallpaper and put on a fresh coat of paint.*

This is exactly why you should seriously think about making any modifications to a rental property. **At the end of your lease, the last thing you want to do is have to rehab your old rental when your attention is primarily focused on moving into your new place.** You *could* always leave your mess behind, but *don't be surprised if you're charged a substantial penalty.*

Reassessing the Property's Condition

Performing the same type of analysis on your property as you should have done when you moved in is *just as important* **now as you move out!** The condition of the property should be *inspected on the last day of your tenancy.* It is recommended that you **either photograph or videotape the premises** and **complete the remaining portion of your assessment of property condition checklist** referred to in **Chapter 5**.

Remember, the landlord will be looking not only for changes to the property that have not been restored to their original condition, but also for **signs of excessive wear and tear. Chapter 9** goes into greater detail regarding **the definition of normal wear and tear** versus **excessive abuse**, as well as **the life expectancy of common items.**

If you fail to document your rental's condition – showing the exact state in which you left it – this enables the landlord to claim almost anything. This isn't just a remark made to protect you from the bad landlords; it's to make sure you have enough ammunition to dispute the more difficult, law-abiding ones. These are the landlords that will find fault with almost anything in the unit, as opposed to lying about the damage or causing it themselves. For this reason, *you may want to accompany the landlord as he or she inspects your unit.* This way, **you'll be able to address or dispute the findings immediately without being confrontational.**

In a worst-case scenario, **if something is found to be wrong, you have every right to request that you be given a chance to be able to correct it** – *as opposed to relying on the landlord to make the repair or to hire someone to do it, either way charging it against your remaining security deposit.*

Just be sure your final walkthrough occurs during the term of your lease – *because once you vacate, the landlord is not obligated to allow you back in to correct the problem.* **More on this topic and the laws** that govern it are **discussed in the next chapter** on security deposits…

Chapter 9

Security Deposits:
How to Get Your Money Back

This Chapter Discusses:

★ **Security Deposit Limits**

★ **The Right to Accrue Interest**

★ **Deadlines for Returning Security Deposits**

★ **The Top Reasons for Losing Your Security Deposit**

★ **Life Expectancy of Common Household Items**

★ **How to Handle a Security Deposit Dispute**

This is by far the most common problem and concern among tenants – *if and when the security deposit will be returned.* As you know, **this is the landlord's primary defense against lease violations;** going to court is a distant second. **Landlords don't like to go to court over matters** *(unless an eviction is necessary)* because of the time and effort involved to take action against a tenant which – if they're lucky – will result in being awarded a judgment that is very difficult to collect.

The security deposit, on the other hand, is something landlords can very easily hold back, as long as they (alone) determine there is just cause to do so. Unfortunately, *the only way for you to refute their decision is to take them to court.* Well, you could always threaten to take your landlord to court, but your landlord could easily stand his or her ground and call your bluff – so you would need to follow through with court action instead of walking away with your tail between your legs. So **this chapter is intended to help you get as much of your security deposit back as you can without enduring too much of an inconvenience.**

Security Deposit Limits

Before learning about how to go about getting your security deposit back into your hands, **it's important to understand the law and the limits imposed** *before* **you even give the landlord a security deposit.** Individual states have their own guidelines and *some states actually have no guidelines at all.* **A state list specifying the maximum amount a landlord can collect as a security deposit** on a residential unit **is presented on the next two pages.** For those states that have no guidelines, it will simply state **"No statute."**

Security Deposit Limits

Alabama	1 month's rent
Alaska	2 months' rent, limit does not apply unless monthly rent exceeds $2,000
Arizona	1 ½ months' rent unless both parties agree to more
Arkansas	2 months' rent
California	2 months' rent if unfurnished unit; 3 months' rent if furnished unit; extra ½ month's rent if tenant has waterbed
Colorado	No statute
Connecticut	2 months' rent, 1 month's rent if tenant is 62 or older
Delaware	No limit if furnished unit or if month-to-month tenancy; 1 month's rent if year or longer lease
District of Columbia	1 month's rent
Florida	No statute
Georgia	No statute
Hawaii	1 month's rent
Idaho	No statute
Illinois	No statute
Indiana	No statute
Iowa	2 months' rent
Kansas	1 month's rent if unfurnished unit; 1 ½ months' rent if furnished unit
Kentucky	No statute
Louisiana	No statute
Maine	2 months' rent
Maryland	2 months' rent
Massachusetts	1 month's rent
Michigan	1 ½ months' rent
Minnesota	No statute
Mississippi	No statute

Missouri	2 months' rent
Montana	No statute
Nebraska	1 month's rent
Nevada	3 months' rent
New Hampshire	$100 or 1 month's rent, whichever greater; no limit if landlord and tenant share facilities
New Jersey	1 ½ months' rent
New Mexico	1 month's rent if less than 1-year lease; no limit if year or longer lease
New York	No limit unless covered by local rent control regulations
North Carolina	1 ½ months' rent if month-to-month tenancy; 2 months' rent if lease term longer than 2 months
North Dakota	1 month's rent
Ohio	No statute
Oklahoma	No statute
Oregon	No statute
Pennsylvania	2 months' rent first year of tenancy; 1 month's rent all future years
Rhode Island	1 month's rent
South Carolina	No statute
South Dakota	1 month's rent
Tennessee	No statute
Texas	No statute
Utah	No statute
Vermont	No statute
Virginia	2 months' rent
Washington	No statute
West Virginia	No statute
Wisconsin	No statute
Wyoming	No statute

If your landlord tries to collect more than what the law of your state allows, don't be afraid to tell the landlord that he or she may be collecting too much according to state law. You can either show the landlord a current copy of this book as a reliable reference (at the time of its publication) or ask him or her to contact your state's equivalent to a department of real estate for clarification.

Remember – this section only applies to money that is intended to be used for security. This is *not to be confused* with the last month's rent or non-refundable pet deposit that your landlord may also collect from you.

The Right to Accrue Interest

The funds you give to the landlord (prior to any claim being made against them) are still your funds and all states recognize this fact – some more than others. Because of the substantial amount of money that you part with for the entire term of your lease, *there are a few states (and even some major cities) that require you to be paid interest* (especially if the landlord is holding your money in an interest-bearing account). The specifics of those states that require you to benefit while your money is taken out of your hands are provided in the following three pages...

Security Deposit Interest Requirements

Alabama	No statute
Alaska	No statute
Arizona	No statute
Arkansas	No statute
California	No statute
Colorado	No statute
Connecticut	Pay annually and at termination, equal to average rate on savings accts at insured banks but not less than 1.5%
Delaware	No statute
District of Columbia	Pay at termination, at current passbook rate
Florida	Not required, but if made must pay annually and at termination; tenant who wrongfully terminates is not entitled to; lease agreement must give details on interest
Georgia	No statute
Hawaii	No statute
Idaho	No statute
Illinois	Required if owner has 25+ properties adjacent to each other or in same building; if security deposit held for longer than 6 months, must pay annually and at termination
Indiana	No statute
Iowa	Not required, but if paid must pay at termination; however, any interest earned during the first 5 years is landlord's
Kansas	No statute
Kentucky	No statute
Louisiana	No statute
Maine	No statute
Maryland	Must pay semi-annually, at a rate of 4% if deposit is greater than $50
Massachusetts	Must pay annually and within 30 days of termination, at a rate of 5% or the actual rate earned; no interest for last month's rent paid in advance
Michigan	No statute

Minnesota	Must pay at a rate of 1%; total interest under $1 does not need to be paid
Mississippi	No statute
Missouri	No statute
Montana	No statute
Nebraska	No statute
Nevada	No statute
New Hampshire	Only required if deposit held for a year or longer; must pay at termination; tenant can request payment every 3 years if request made within 30 days of tenancy expiration/renewal; rate must be equal to the rate paid on the bank savings account where deposited
New Jersey	Must pay annually or credit back to rent owed; landlord with less than 10 units can put deposit in any insured interest-bearing bank account; those with 10 or more must put funds in an insured money market account that matures in a year or less or in any other account that pays interest at a comparable rate to a money market account
New Mexico	Must pay annually at rate equal to passbook rate if deposit is more than 1 month's rent and there is a year lease
New York	Must pay at prevailing rate if unit is covered under rent control or stabilization requirements or if building has 6 or more units; landlord can keep 1% admin fee a year
North Carolina	No statute
North Dakota	Must pay interest if tenancy is at least 9 months; deposit must be put in an insured interest-bearing savings or checking acct
Ohio	Must pay annually and at termination, at a rate of 5% if the tenancy is 6 months or more and the deposit is greater than $50 or 1 month's rent - whichever is greater - the interest only accrues on the excess of the $50 or 1-month-rent amount
Oklahoma	No statute
Oregon	No statute
Pennsylvania	Must pay if tenancy is longer than 2 years; interest accrues from start of 25th month of tenancy and must be paid annually after that point; landlord can deduct 1% fee
Rhode Island	No statute
South Carolina	No statute
South Dakota	No statute
Tennessee	No statute

Texas	No statute
Utah	No statute
Vermont	No statute
Virginia	Must pay if deposit is held for more than 13 months for continued tenancy in same unit; interest accrues from start of lease and must be paid at termination; must be at rate of 1% below FED discount rate as of Jan. 1 of each year
Washington	No statute
West Virginia	No statute
Wisconsin	No statute
Wyoming	No statute

Deadlines for Returning Security Deposits

This section applies to **the amount of time that your landlord has to return the security deposit** he or she collected from you. Even though there are many states that do not impose security deposit limits, **most of them require the landlord to give the deposit back –** regardless of the amount – **within a certain period of time.** This is an important aspect of your state's law to understand because *if the landlord fails to return your security deposit without providing you notice and itemizing why it was withheld* (e.g., damages, unpaid rent), *he or she can be ordered by a court to pay you a penalty in most cases.*

Even some local jurisdictions have laws in place to protect you that take precedence over what the state has to say about such matters. In **Chicago**, for instance, a tenant can be awarded up to the equivalent of two times the security deposit should the landlord violate just one of many sections of the Windy City's **Residential Landlord Tenant Ordinance (RLTO).**

While this may seem incredibly obvious, **the number one reason why tenants do not receive their security deposit back** within a reasonable amount of time is *failure to provide a forwarding address.* Ridiculous isn't it? But many tenants forget to tell their landlord where they moved to… So **in order to get your security deposit back, you must provide your landlord with a new mailing address!**

CAUTION

This is not to say that you should haggle your landlord to death. However, you do have rights and when it comes to security deposits – **this is your money, not the landlord's.** In the end, it will be up to you regarding whether to pursue legal action to punish your landlord. Fortunately, **most cases concerning security deposits can be taken care of in a small claims court,** which does not require (or even allow) legal representation in order to keep matters simple. **As long as you have adequate proof justifying your position by showing how your rights were violated, you will greatly improve your chances of prevailing.**

While this book would love to attempt to address every local jurisdiction in the United States, it's just not possible. **The laws being summarized are done so at the state level.** Therefore, *there may be (albeit in limited circumstances) local ordinances that supersede your state's guidelines.* As always, **you should contact your local government housing offices and inquire about any special rules or regulations that would affect your particular situation.** In the meantime, **a summary of each state's deadlines for returning security deposits appears on the next two pages.**

Deadlines for Returning Security Deposits

Alabama	35 days
Alaska	14 days if proper termination notice given; 30 days if not
Arizona	14 days
Arkansas	30 days
California	21 days
Colorado	1 month unless lease provides for longer period up to 60 days; 72 weekday non-holiday hours if emergency termination due to gas equipment hazard
Connecticut	30 days or within 15 days of receipt of forwarding address from tenant, whichever is later
Delaware	20 days
District of Columbia	45 days
Florida	15 days if no deductions; 30 days to give notice of what deductions will be made; then tenant has 15 days to dispute any deduction and remaining deposit must be returned within 30 days of initial deduction notification
Georgia	1 month
Hawaii	14 days
Idaho	21 days unless both parties agree; then up to 30 days
Illinois	45 days if no deductions; 30 days to itemize deductions
Indiana	45 days
Iowa	30 days
Kansas	30 days
Kentucky	No statute deadline for returning; if the tenant leaves owing the last month's rent and does not request their security deposit back, the landlord may apply the security deposit to the rent owed after 30 days; if the tenant leaves owing no rent and having a refund due to them, the landlord must send an itemization to the tenant; but if the tenant does not respond to the landlord after 60 days, the landlord may keep the deposit
Louisiana	1 month
Maine	21 days if tenancy at will; 30 days if written lease
Maryland	45 days; 10 days to itemize deductions if tenant utilizes a surety bond
Massachusetts	30 days

Michigan	30 days
Minnesota	3 weeks; 5 days if termination due to condemnation
Mississippi	45 days
Missouri	30 days
Montana	10 days if no deductions; 30 days if deductions
Nebraska	14 days
Nevada	30 days
New Hampshire	30 days; if shared facilities and deposit is more than 30 days' rent, then 20 days unless written agreement otherwise
New Jersey	30 days; 5 days if termination due to fire, flood, condemnation, evacuation; deadline does not apply if property is owner-occupied and has only 1 or 2 units if the tenant did not provide a written 30 days notification to the landlord of their desire to invoke the law
New Mexico	30 days
New York	Reasonable time
North Carolina	30 days
North Dakota	30 days
Ohio	30 days
Oklahoma	30 days
Oregon	31 days
Pennsylvania	30 days
Rhode Island	20 days
South Carolina	30 days
South Dakota	2 weeks to return deposit and/or provide explanation for any withholding; 45 days to provide an itemized accounting of all deductions made to the security deposit if the tenant requests one
Tennessee	No statute; 10 days to itemize deductions
Texas	30 days
Utah	30 days or within 15 days of receipt of forwarding address from tenant, whichever is later
Vermont	14 days

Virginia	45 days
Washington	14 days
West Virginia	No statute
Wisconsin	21 days
Wyoming	30 days or within 15 days of receipt of forwarding address from tenant, whichever is later; 60 days if unit has damage

The Top Reasons for Losing Your Security Deposit

Without going into great detail to try and explain a rare breed of eccentric landlords that nickel and dime their tenants to death, **this section will sum up the most common reasons why tenants lose some or all of their security deposits.** Don't be so quick to dismiss the obvious ones, because anyone can forget even the simplest of things. So **here are the most common reasons why tenants lose some or all of their security deposits...**

The Most Common Reasons Why Security Deposits Are Lost:

☆ Failing to Give Proper Notice

Prior to leaving, **some state's deposit laws require you to give written notice to the landlord.** These notice requirements vary from 30 to 60 days and are intended to prevent misunderstandings about your departure date and how much rent is owed (should it need to be prorated). *A common mistake for some tenants in those jurisdictions that require advance notice to be given is to assume that when the lease is up, they can simply leave.* **The landlord may keep up to the equivalent of one month's rent in certain jurisdictions** (e.g., Houston) **if you fail to give written notice before vacating.** Just remember (regardless of where you live and the laws governing your tenancy) – *it doesn't cost a thing to give a written notice.*

⭐ Unpaid Rent

Leaving early or breaking a lease altogether can cause your security deposit to be forfeited to cover the remaining amount due. If possible (as discussed in **Chapter 12**) *you should try to avoid early termination by finding a suitable replacement to take your spot.* **Otherwise, you could be legally responsible until the vacancy is filled or the lease expires.** Therefore, it's possible you could be held liable for several months, depending on when you leave.

⭐ Cleaning Fee

"But it wasn't clean when I moved in…" **This is why you need to complain to the landlord immediately upon moving in if it isn't clean or at least capture its condition on some photographic medium** – *because when you move out, it's too late.* **If the unit isn't returned in its original condition, the deposit may be used to mop up the mess.**

It's best to ask your landlord what his or her expectations are regarding this very issue when you first move in. If not, you should at least give the landlord a call before you move out **to find out if there are any specific demands.** Some landlords consider "clean" to be just removing your personal possessions, while others expect the carpet to be shampooed and the bathrooms disinfected with bleach.

⭐ Failing to Restore to Its Original Condition

This is a hotly contested issue on both sides of the fence. Remember – **any modifications to the rental unit have to be reverted to their original state** *unless* **your landlord agrees to accept the changes you've made.** This is why it's always best to ask the landlord about your proposed modifications and whether he or she will accept them or require you to restore the unit upon moving out. **You should then ask yourself if all of this work is really necessary and could you instead accept the unit "as-is…"**

★ Damage

Think of damage as injury to the premises that goes *beyond* **normal wear and tear.** The basic principle behind "normal wear and tear" is to expect to see some minor cosmetic blemishes that occur naturally with time, when used in accordance with manufacturers' recommendations. **Appliances, fixtures and hardware throughout the rental are all expected to be left in working order, devoid of obvious abuse or neglect.** The longer you lease an apartment, the more wear and tear is expected, especially for carpeting and paint – **just be sure to document everything.** *Damage is usually caused by a spontaneous event* – such as spilt coffee or a ball thrown inside the house – and *it needs to be taken care of before you move out.*

★ Missing Items

To take or not to take? If the unit was rented with the coolest little light fixtures, make sure they're still there when you perform your end-of-lease inspection. Yes, **even potted plants and lawn furnishings must stay – they are not yours to keep!** Once again, this is obvious – but everyone knows of someone whose prized salt and pepper shakers came from his or her favorite restaurant…

Life Expectancy of Common Household Items

There is, to some extent, a general consensus about the life expectancy of certain household items that should be understood – so you can protect yourself in case you are blamed for an item's poor condition when it was already well past its prime. This section *applies not only to the interior, but exterior elements too.* While it may be true that many items can still thrive well beyond what is mentioned here, **you should not be held responsible for any excessive wear and tear beyond an item's normal limits...**

Life Expectancy of Common Household Items

Bathtub	20 years
Bathroom Flooring	10 years
Bathroom Sink	17 years
Carpeting	10 years
Closet Doors (Folding)	8 years
Curtain Rods	8 years
Curtains	5 years
Dishwasher	10 years
Door Hardware	15 years
Drapes	10 years
Exhaust Fan	3 years
Exterior Doors	15 years
Exterior Paint	6 years
Faucets	8 years
Garbage Disposal	5 years
Hot Water Heater	10 years
Interior Doors	20 years
Kitchen Cabinets	15 years
Kitchen Flooring	12 years
Kitchen Sink	17 years
Medicine Cabinet	12 years
Range	12 years
Range Hood	9 years
Refrigerator	15 years
Screens and Frames	5 years
Toilet	20 years

Toilet Float and Trim	7 years
Towel Bar	5 years
Window Hardware	15 years

How to Handle a Security Deposit Dispute

Depending on how often you move, **you'll probably take issue with your landlord at some point or another regarding your security deposit.** You may even be unlucky enough to get into a disagreement the first time you rent. *The important thing is how to handle the matter.* **Communication is the key to avoiding and resolving problems.** Your landlord may be willing to work out a solution. *Both of you should bear in mind that each has the duty to deal with the other fairly and in good faith.* If the problem truly cannot be resolved by discussion, negotiation and acceptable compromise, then you can look to the remedies provided by the law. But **before you pursue your legal remedies, be sure to read this section thoroughly.**

There are essentially two scenarios that this section will deal with... The first is *when a landlord provides you with an itemized statement regarding deductions he or she made against your security deposit.* Remember, **security deposits can be used for any of the following:**

★ A Summary of How a Security Deposit Can Lawfully Be Used:

- **To reserve the premises** before a tenant takes occupancy

- **To cover the unpaid portion of rent** if the tenant abandons the residence

- To compensate for **unpaid utility bills**

- **To pay for damages beyond normal wear and tear** *("Normal wear and tear" is defined as* "deterioration which occurs based upon the use for which the rental unit is intended without negligence, carelessness, accident or abuse of the premises or equipment by the tenant or his/her guests")

- **Any other breach of the lease causing damage**

If you disagree with any of the items provided by the landlord, then a letter should be immediately mailed to the landlord addressing your concerns. This is a good time to **include those photographic images you should have taken prior to vacating** and the **checklist that was completed on the last day of your tenancy.** A **sample letter has been provided on the next page for your use.** This letter is *intended only as a guide* and *should be elaborated* to better explain your own *personal circumstances.*

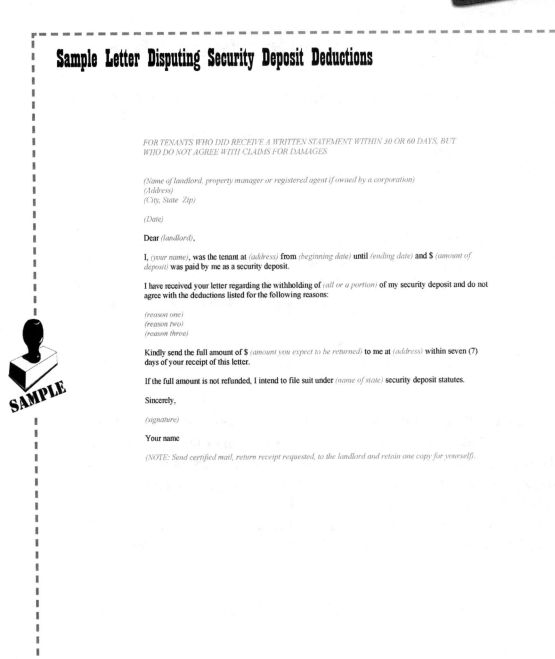

Sample Letter Disputing Security Deposit Deductions

FOR TENANTS WHO DID RECEIVE A WRITTEN STATEMENT WITHIN 30 OR 60 DAYS, BUT WHO DO NOT AGREE WITH CLAIMS FOR DAMAGES.

(Name of landlord, property manager or registered agent if owned by a corporation)
(Address)
(City, State Zip)

(Date)

Dear *(landlord)*,

I, *(your name)*, was the tenant at *(address)* from *(beginning date)* until *(ending date)* and $ *(amount of deposit)* was paid by me as a security deposit.

I have received your letter regarding the withholding of *(all or a portion)* of my security deposit and do not agree with the deductions listed for the following reasons:

(reason one)
(reason two)
(reason three)

Kindly send the full amount of $ *(amount you expect to be returned)* to me at *(address)* within seven (7) days of your receipt of this letter.

If the full amount is not refunded, I intend to file suit under *(name of state)* security deposit statutes.

Sincerely,

(signature)

Your name

(NOTE: Send certified mail, return receipt requested, to the landlord and retain one copy for yourself).

SAMPLE

The second scenario focuses on what you do if the landlord fails to give you any explanation or fails to return any of your security deposit. If this is the case, then you need to write a different letter. This letter not only should address your concern about not receiving any correspondence at all when you've provided a valid forwarding address, but should *also* reference whatever your state's law may be regarding the deadline for returning your security deposit.

Once again, **the sample letter provided on the next page should be embellished** by citing your state (or local) laws, as well as anything else that may be relevant.

Sample Letter for No Landlord Correspondence or Money

FOR TENANTS WHO DID NOT RECEIVE A WRITTEN STATEMENT (OR THE ENTIRE SECURITY DEPOSIT) WITHIN 30 OR 60 DAYS OF MOVING OUT.

(Name of landlord, property manager or registered agent if owned by a corporation)
(Address)
(City, State Zip)

(Date)

Dear *(landlord)*,

I, *(your name)*, was the tenant at *(address)* from *(beginning date)* until *(ending date)* and $ *(amount of deposit)* was paid by me as a security deposit.

It has been more than *(30 or 60 days)* since I moved out on *(ending date)*.

I have received neither a written explanation nor the return of my deposit.

Kindly send the full amount of $ *(amount you expect to be returned)* to me at *(address)* within seven (7) days of your receipt of this letter.

If the full amount is not refunded, I intend to file suit under *(name of state)* security deposit statutes.

Sincerely,

(signature)

Your name

(NOTE: Send certified mail, return receipt requested, to the landlord and retain one copy for yourself).

SAMPLE

If you are unable to get anywhere with your landlord and it appears he or she may have violated the law, then you should contact any one of the following third parties to seek their free advice or assistance. Of course, you can always hire a local real estate attorney, but security deposit issues can often be handled with a little bit of assistance from any of the following housing agencies or departments listed below. **Ultimately, you can take your landlord to small claims court by paying a small filing fee** (usually no more than $100).

Whom to Contact Regarding a Security Deposit Dispute:

 Local Consumer Protection Agency

See the City and County Government listings in the white pages of the phone book.

 Local Housing Agency

See the City and County Government listings in the white pages of the phone book.

 Local District Attorney's Office

See the City and County Government listings in the white pages of the phone book.

 City or County Rent Control Board *(if applicable)*

See the City and County Government listings in the white pages of the phone book.

 Local Tenant or Apartment Association

See the yellow pages of the phone book.

Chapter 10

Basic Tenant Rights:
A Safe, Secure and Enjoyable Place to Rent

This Chapter Discusses:

- ★ Privacy
- ★ Security
- ★ Noisy Neighbors
- ★ Habitable Living Conditions
- ★ Discrimination
- ★ How and Where to Get Help

A long with the common monetary issues that have been discussed so far – such as rent control, rent increases, security deposits and late payments – **every tenant is subsequently entitled to a set of basic rights, regardless of where he or she decides to rent a place to live.** This chapter provides **an overview of each of these rights,** along with **tips on how to handle their respective violations.**

Privacy

Next to disputes over rent and security deposits, **the tenant's right to privacy and the landlord's right to enter the premises is the third most commonly contested issue.** Obviously, *you have the right to be left alone* (in most instances). However, as you could appreciate, the landlord has rights as well. Not to peek into your windows, but **to legally enter rented premises in cases of emergency, in order to make needed repairs** (in some states, just to determine whether repairs are necessary) **or to show the property to prospective tenants** or purchasers.

Several states even allow landlords the right of entry during a tenant's extended absence (often defined as **seven days or more) to maintain the property as necessary** and to inspect for damage and needed repairs. Fortunately, *in most cases, a landlord may not enter just to check up on the tenant and the rental property.* **States typically require landlords to provide advance notice (usually 24 hours) before entering a rental unit.** Without advance notice, a landlord or manager may enter rented premises while a tenant is living there *only in an emergency* – such as a fire or serious water leak, or when you give your permission. A **summary of each state's law pertaining to how much notice of entry is needed in non-emergency situations** is **provided on the next two pages.**

Notice of Entry Requirements

Alabama	2 days
Alaska	24 hours
Arizona	2 days
Arkansas	Not specified
California	24 hours; 48 hours if preliminary inspection
Colorado	No statute
Connecticut	Reasonable time
Delaware	2 days
District of Columbia	No statute
Florida	12 hours
Georgia	No statute
Hawaii	2 days
Idaho	No statute
Illinois	No statute
Indiana	Reasonable time
Iowa	24 hours
Kansas	Reasonable time
Kentucky	2 days
Louisiana	No statute
Maine	24 hours
Maryland	No statute
Massachusetts	Not specified
Michigan	No statute
Minnesota	Reasonable time
Mississippi	No statute
Missouri	No statute

Montana	24 hours
Nebraska	1 day
Nevada	24 hours
New Hampshire	Adequate notice for the circumstance
New Jersey	No statute
New Mexico	24 hours
New York	No statute
North Carolina	No statute
North Dakota	Reasonable time
Ohio	24 hours
Oklahoma	1 day
Oregon	24 hours
Pennsylvania	No statute
Rhode Island	2 days
South Carolina	24 hours
South Dakota	No statute
Tennessee	Not specified
Texas	No statute
Utah	Not specified
Vermont	24 hours
Virginia	24 hours
Washington	2 days
West Virginia	No statute
Wisconsin	Advanced notice, unless lease provides time frame
Wyoming	No statute

Security

Landlords are responsible for your safety and security to a degree. Most states **require landlords to protect you from potential criminals** – *especially those crimes that may be committed by neighboring tenants.* Landlords are also **partially responsible for protecting their local community from any illegal activities engaged in by their tenants,** such as drug dealing, prostitution and acts of violence.

Fortunately, over the years, **tenants and the communities have complained and continue to complain about particular occurrences that have brought about new laws to enforce this important right of security.** Here is a list of **some basic things that a landlord** *must* **do in order to protect you.**

☆ How a Landlord Must Protect a Tenant:

♦ Every **landlord must comply with all state and local security laws that apply to residential rental property** by providing **deadbolt locks on doors, adequate lighting** and **window locks.**

♦ Assess the crime situation in and around the rental property and neighborhood and **design a security system that provides reasonable protection for you inside and outside the rental unit** – including common areas found in apartment communities.

♦ **Inform tenants about known criminal activity in the area** and **describe the security measures provided by the landlord** and their limitations or vulnerabilities.

♦ **Conduct regular inspections to ensure all security items are functioning normally** – and if not, *fix those problems*, such as broken locks or poor lighting conditions.

♦ **Respond to tenant complaints about dangerous situations, suspicious activities or broken security items immediately.** *Failing to take tenant issues seriously could result in a landlord being faced with a higher degree of legal liability, should someone get injured.*

Noisy Neighbors

Noisy neighbors are a nationwide epidemic. They're everywhere. The question is: how do you handle a situation when your neighbor is playing music too loud at 2:30AM – or your neighbor's dog is barking and just won't shut up? If you're renting a house, it won't do you any good to call your landlord unless the neighboring house is also one of his or her rental properties.

So, **the first step is to talk to your neighbor in the most polite manner possible.** Having a heated discussion will not solve anything and may just make matters worse. **Believe it or not, it's quite possible that the neighbor may not even realize how loud he or she is and it may only take one short phone call or personal visit to get some peace and quiet.**

If your neighbor fails to accommodate your friendly request and the problem persists, then **your second step is to call the police or sheriff's department and file a complaint.** Unfortunately, **there's not much that local law enforcement can do unless the neighbor is still noisy when the law enforcement officer shows up.** Fortunately, the mere presence of a man or woman with a badge and a holstered gun does the trick all by itself.

As a last resort, after you've contacted the neighbor and called the police to no avail, **you'll have no choice but to take your neighbor to small claims court and sue** for lost sleep, pain and suffering and whatever else you can come up with. **Just make sure you've documented all of your correspondence** with your neighbor, the police department and any witnesses.

If you happen to live in an **apartment complex**, the **resolution is usually much easier, so long as your complaints are valid and the landlord is responsive.** You should **first communicate with your neighbor politely and let the person know that the noise is bothersome.** If the problem then continues, **provide your landlord with as much information as possible.** Hopefully, you'll have **a list of fellow neighbors who will concur with you.** *The more you can bring to the table, the better your chances of getting the landlord to follow through and resolve the problem* without you having to take the noisy neighbor *and* your landlord to small claims court.

The most important thing to remember from this section is to **make sure you come across as the well-composed victim who's never irate or irrational.** It's always best for you to **maintain a serious but reasonable demeanor**, so that you can get results without losing anyone's respect.

Habitable Living Conditions

As a tenant, **you are entitled to rent a place that does not materially affect your health and safety.** In other words, *the unit must be habitable in compliance with all state and local building and health codes.* **Landlords are the ones ultimately legally responsible for assuring that their rental units are habitable.** Therefore, *they are responsible for*  *maintaining and repairing significant defects in the rental unit and substantial failures to comply with state and local building and health codes.* **However, landlords are not financially responsible for repairing damages that were caused by tenants, their family, guests and pets.**

Tenants are required to take reasonable care of their rental units, as well as any common areas, such as recreation rooms, lobbies and any outside areas. **Tenants are responsible for repairing all damage that results from their neglect or abuse –** and for **damage caused by family members, guests or pets.**

Most laws are very specific as to what kinds of conditions make a rental uninhabitable. **All jurisdictions consider a rental unit to be uninhabitable if it contains a lead hazard that endangers the occupants or the public** or is a *substandard building* or a **nuisance that endangers the health, life, safety, property or welfare of the occupants or the general public.** In addition, **most jurisdictions will also require the landlord to ensure each rental has the following list of essential items:**

★ Landlord Responsibilities for Maintaining a Habitable Rental Unit:

- ♦ Effective **waterproofing and weather protection of roof and exterior walls,** including **unbroken windows and doors.**

- ♦ **Plumbing facilities in good working order,** including **hot and cold running water,** connected to a **sewage disposal system.**

- ♦ **Gas facilities** in good working order (if applicable).

- ♦ **Heating facilities** in good working order.

- ♦ An **electrical system,** including **lighting, wiring** and **requisite equipment,** in good working order.

- ♦ **Clean and sanitary buildings and grounds** that are **free from debris, filth, rubbish, garbage, rodents and vermin.**

- ♦ **Adequate trash receptacles** in good repair.

- ♦ **Floors, stairways** and **railings** in good repair.

- ♦ A **working toilet, wash basin** and **bathtub or shower.** The toilet and bathtub or shower **must be in a room that is ventilated and allows privacy.**

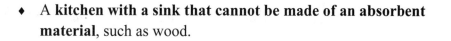

- A **kitchen with a sink that cannot be made of an absorbent material**, such as wood.

- **Natural lighting in every room through windows or skylights.** Windows in each room **must be able to open at least half-way for ventilation**, unless a **fan provides mechanical ventilation**.

- **Safe fire or emergency exits leading to a street or hallway.** Stairs, hallways and exits **must be kept litter-free.** Storage areas, garages and basements must be kept **free of combustible materials.**

- **Operable deadbolt locks on the main entry doors of rental units** and **operable locking or security devices on windows.**

- **Working smoke detectors in all units of multi-unit buildings,** such as duplexes and apartment complexes. Apartment complexes also **must have smoke detectors in common stairwells.**

- **Ground fault circuit interrupters for swimming pools** and **anti-suction protections for wading pools** in apartment complexes and other residential settings (but not single-family residences).

A landlord is not responsible for providing aesthetically pleasing conditions. Nor is he or she responsible for any violations of housing codes that are considered minor and do not affect the habitability of the property.

In addition to having to take reasonable care of the rental unit, **you as the tenant are also responsible for maintaining the habitability of the unit.** *If you fail to live up to the responsibilities listed on the next page, you cannot withhold rent or sue the landlord for providing an uninhabitable place to live.*

★ Tenant Responsibilities for Maintaining a Habitable Rental Unit:

♦ To keep the premises **"as clean and sanitary as the condition of the premises permits."**

♦ **To use and operate gas, electrical and plumbing fixtures properly.** (Examples of improper use include overloading electrical outlets; flushing large, foreign objects down the toilet; and allowing any gas, electrical or plumbing fixture to become filthy.)

♦ **To dispose of trash and garbage in a clean and sanitary manner.**

♦ **Not to destroy, damage, or deface the premises** – or allow anyone else to do so either.

♦ **Not to remove any part of the structure, dwelling unit, facilities, equipment or appurtenances** – or allow anyone else to do so.

♦ **To use the premises as a place to live** – and **use the rooms for their intended purposes.** For example, the bedroom must be used as a bedroom, not as a kitchen.

♦ **To notify the landlord when** deadbolt locks and window locks or **security devices don't operate properly.**

Other kinds of repairs or maintenance issues that are considered less serious **can be either the landlord's or tenant's responsibility**, *depending on how the lease agreement is written.* Therefore, it's important to negotiate your lease agreement based upon the types of repairs you're willing to make.

Discrimination

A landlord cannot refuse to rent to a tenant or harass him or her because of the person's race, color, religion, sex (including *pregnancy*, *childbirth* or *medical conditions* related to gender and perception of gender), **sexual orientation, marital status, national origin, ancestry, familial status, source of income or disability.** Here is a **summary of what most jurisdictions prohibit landlords from discriminating against**:

☆ Landlords Cannot Discriminate Against:

- A person's because of a **medical condition** or **mental or physical disability**.

- **Personal characteristics**, such as a *person's physical appearance* or *sexual orientation,* that are not related to the responsibilities of a tenant.

- A person because of a **perception of a person's race, color, religion, sex, sexual orientation, marital status, national origin, ancestry, familial status, source of income, disability or medical conditions** – or a *perception that a person is associated with another person who may have any of these characteristics.*

- **Persons who want to live together** and **combine their incomes,** *as opposed to married persons who combine their incomes,* **by using a** *different* **financial or income standard for each.** In the case of a **government rent subsidy**, a landlord who is assessing a potential tenant's eligibility for a rental unit *must use a financial or income standard that is based on the portion of rent that the tenant would pay.* A landlord cannot apply rules, regulations or policies to **unmarried couples** who are **registered domestic partners** that do not *apply to married couples.*

♦ **Families with children under 18.** However, *housing for senior citizens may exclude families with children.* **"Housing for senior citizens"** includes a retirement community that is **occupied only by persons who are at least age 55.**

Unlawful housing discrimination can take a variety of forms. **Here is a list of some common examples of discriminatory acts performed by landlords:**

★ Examples of Discriminatory Acts Performed by Landlords:

♦ **Refusing to sell, rent, or lease.**

♦ **Refusing to negotiate** for a sale, rental, or lease.

♦ **Representing that housing is not available** for inspection, sale or rental **when it, in fact, is.**

♦ Otherwise **denying or withholding housing accommodations.**

♦ **Providing inferior** housing terms, conditions, privileges, facilities or services.

♦ **Harassing a person in connection with housing accommodations**.

♦ **Canceling or terminating** a sale or rental agreement.

♦ **Providing segregated or separated** housing accommodations.

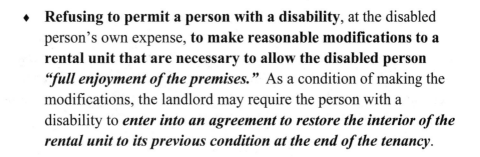

♦ **Refusing to permit a person with a disability**, at the disabled person's own expense, **to make reasonable modifications to a rental unit that are necessary to allow the disabled person** *"full enjoyment of the premises."* As a condition of making the modifications, the landlord may require the person with a disability to *enter into an agreement to restore the interior of the rental unit to its previous condition at the end of the tenancy*.

♦ **Refusing to make reasonable accommodations in rules, policies, practices or services when necessary to allow a person with a disability** *"equal opportunity to use and enjoy a dwelling"* (for example, refusing to allow a person with a disability a companion or service dog on a "no pets" contract).

How and Where to Get Help

If you are ever a victim of housing discrimination, there are several legal remedies available to you under most state and local laws. A summary of the remedies is provided below.

★ Common Legal Remedies for Discrimination:

♦ **Recovery of out-of-pocket losses**

♦ An **injunction prohibiting the unlawful practice**

♦ **Access to housing** that the landlord denied you

♦ **Damages for emotional distress**

♦ **Civil penalties or punitive damages**

♦ **Attorney fees**

You must act quickly if you believe that a landlord has unlawfully discriminated against you. The time-limits for filing housing discrimination complaints may be *as short as one year* from the date of the incident. So *as soon as the discriminatory act occurs, be sure to document everything* by writing down what happened, including dates and the names of those involved – and **then, contact one of the resources listed below for advice and help.**

Whom to Contact When Discriminated Against:

☆ **Local Fair Housing Organizations (Fair Housing Councils)**
Look in the white (business) and yellow pages of the phone book.

☆ **Local State Apartment Association Chapters**
Look in the white (business) and yellow pages of the phone book.

☆ **Local Government Agencies**
Look in the white pages of the phone book under City or County Government Offices – or call the offices of local elected officials (for example, your city council representative or your county supervisor).

☆ **U.S. Department of Housing and Urban Development (HUD)**
HUD enforces the *federal fair housing law*, which **prohibits discrimination based on sex, race, color, religion, national origin, familial status or disability.** To contact **HUD**, look in the white pages of the phone book under United States Government Offices, or go to **www.hud.gov**.

☆ **Legal Aid Organizations**
These organizations provide *free legal advice*, *representation* and *other legal services* in non-criminal cases **to economically disadvantaged persons**. Legal aid organizations are *located throughout each state*. Look in the yellow pages **under Attorneys**.

★ Private Attorneys

You may be able to hire a private attorney to take legal action against a landlord who has discriminated against you. **For the names of attorneys who specialize in housing discrimination cases,** *call your county bar association or an attorney referral service.*

Chapter 11

Minor Maintenance and Repairs: Getting the Small Jobs Taken Care Of

This Chapter Discusses:

★ Who's Responsible for What?
★ Provide a Written Request
★ Taking Action Against Your Landlord
★ Filing a Small Claims Lawsuit

As discussed in **Chapter 10, your landlord is responsible for keeping the property in a habitable condition.** *But what about the minor problems, like leaky faucets, old paint, torn wallpaper, broken glass or cracked tiles?* While these types of problems can be bothersome or unsightly, they don't make the unit uninhabitable. As mentioned earlier, **aesthetics play no part when looking at a rental property through the eyes of the law.** Consequently, **this chapter focuses on determining who's actually responsible** *and how to get the job done* within the parameters allowed under state and local laws.

Who's Responsible for What?

Major repairs must be performed by your landlord in most circumstances, because these types of repairs usually have a direct impact on habitable living conditions. **Whether or not your landlord must take care of a minor repair depends** upon a number of factors, beginning with the **nature of the problem.** *Purely cosmetic repairs to your rental are not legally required.* Mildewed caulking around a sink or bathtub, for example, is less likely to require your landlord's attention than a broken drain or cracked tile… that may cause a water leak into the unit and even adjacent units. **In order to determine who is responsible, you'll need to review the following list:**

★ Items That Determine Who's Responsible for Repairs:

- ♦ **Repair clause** found in the **lease agreement**

- ♦ **Previous oral or written promises** made by your landlord

- ♦ State and local **building code requirements**

- ♦ **Local housing authority**

- ♦ State **health department**

- ♦ State and local **landlord-tenant laws**

Provide a Written Request

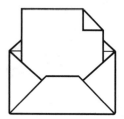

As you know, **talking with your landlord is often the best way to address any type of problem** – but if you've been unsuccessful in the past and/or feel reluctant to do so now, then **your best bet is to document your request in writing and deliver it to the landlord** (and always be sure to retain a copy for your own personal records, as well as documentation of the letter's delivery!). Even if you've already determined that the responsibility may very well be yours, *it doesn't hurt to go ahead and ask your landlord to take care of the problem anyway.* He or she either may have forgotten about any prior agreements or **may even prefer to handle this particular problem** – instead of allowing you to take a shot at it. After all, **it's the landlord's property** and some (more than others) just like to **handle matters themselves as opposed to letting others meddle with their property.**

The nice thing about a letter is that **it gives you a chance to formally present the problem and argue why you believe it's the landlord's responsibility – or at least why it's in his or her best interest to take care of it.** A letter, more so than a conversation, *bears a little more weight because it is perceived to be a serious attempt at communicating* – which may even prompt reluctant landlords to give your request some serious thought instead of giving an immediate "No!" if approached in person; still there are some who would argue that it may be more difficult for the landlord to say "no" in person. Regardless, **the point of the letter is to document the problem and when you brought it to your landlord's attention** – *just in case this turns into more of a problem down the road.*

When drafting your letter, **try to make as many of the following points as you can** (when applicable), because *these will improve your chances of getting the problem resolved quickly.*

By the way, don't waste your time on smoke detector batteries. While the landlord is required to provide the smoke detector, the maintenance (e.g., replacing the batteries) is usually your responsibility. Now, if the unit isn't working at all, then that's the landlord's responsibility to fix it.

☆ Important Points to Make Regarding Your Needed Repair:

- ♦ The **problem may become worse** if it's not taken care of immediately.

- ♦ There is the **potential for injury.**

♦ The problem poses a **security risk.**

♦ The problem may **affect other tenants** or neighbors.

After delivering your letter, **you should allow about 30 days (in non-emergency situations) for your landlord to schedule and perform your repair.** As long as you've been a good tenant and have been performing your own required duties satisfactorily (such as keeping the unit clean, taking care of the appliances and paying the rent on time), you'll find that your landlord will usually be glad to do his or her part in maintaining a healthy relationship with you. After all, *you could choose to live someplace else.*

Taking Action Against Your Landlord

This is when **you have to determine if the minor repair item is worth fighting for or taking action against the landlord.** Keep in mind that *reporting your landlord or taking an adverse action against him or her won't improve your relationship –* which may be important to you if you want to stay in your unit for some time. **Even state "anti-retaliation" laws**, which prohibit rent hikes, lease terminations or other adverse actions following a tenant's complaint to a government agency or exercise of a legal right, **cannot prevent a landlord from making your remaining tenancy very uncomfortable.**

You should seriously consider the nature and severity of the problem before you determine how far you are willing to go. If the problem may violate local building or housing codes, **call the agency that enforces these codes in your area** to find out. A representative at the agency should be able to explain *whether or not your problem in fact violates local or state codes*, and *may be able to take action against your landlord on your behalf.*

If a landlord doesn't meet his or her legal responsibilities, you can usually take any of the following actions, depending on whether your state or local laws permit them.

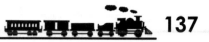
★ Common Retaliatory Actions Taken by Tenants:

♦ **Pay less rent.**

♦ **Withhold the entire rent** until the problem is fixed.

♦ **Hire someone to make necessary repairs** and **deduct the cost from the next month's rent.**

♦ **Call the local building inspector**, who can usually order the landlord to make repairs.

♦ Receive a **partial refund of previously paid rent.**

♦ **Sue your landlord in small claims court for the emotional distress caused by the substandard conditions** (this is *obviously rare* and is *usually reserved for major repairs*).

It is important to note that before you decide to withhold any portion of your rent, *you must confirm with both your state and local housing laws that you are entitled to take such a drastic action.* And remember, **this will certainly create a kink in your relationship with your landlord.** But *if the battle is worth fighting,* then by all means *stand up for your rights* – because your landlord would only do the same with an unresponsive tenant.

Filing a Small Claims Lawsuit

If you must escalate your situation to the **highest level**, this is typically it. While you can always **hire a mediator** to hear both sides, this **seldom happens** because the landlord probably won't cooperate unless he or she is forced to respond by being summoned to court. Most states provide courts at the county level in which individuals may settle small money disputes in an informal and expeditious setting, known as a **small claims court.**

A **small claims court** is **a judicial forum for civil cases that only involve monetary awards of usually $5,000 or less. The small claims court cannot order your landlord to repair your rental unit.** However, *the court can order the landlord to reimburse you for repairs, a portion of your rent and emotional distress.*

Before you bother filing, just make sure you know you're going to win. In other words, don't bother going forward unless you've *checked out the facts of your case against your state and local laws ahead of time.* Once you take your landlord to court, **he or she can always file a counter claim against you and win** *(especially if you've held back your rent or failed to make repairs that were your responsibility).* It certainly wouldn't be to your benefit to go to court unprepared and try to sue your landlord for $500 if he or she could prove that you actually owe him or her $1,000.

To file your case, contact your local county courthouse and ask for the small claims clerk. He or she will be able to provide you with the details of how to file and the fees involved. **You will not be able to do this over the telephone, but at least you'll know in advance what you must be prepared to do when you show up in person to file.** Generally, **you will need to provide the following information when you file your lawsuit:**

☆ Common Information Required to File a Small Claims Lawsuit:

- Your complete **name, address(es)** and **phone number(s).**

- The **complete name and address of the landlord or business entity your claim is against.** *Correct names and addresses are vital to your case,* because the court cannot grant a judgment against a defendant who is improperly named in the complaint. You need to provide **the exact business name and mailing address** *as it appears in your lease agreement.* So if the landlord operates under a business name such as XYZ Property Management, LLC, then that is the exact name you must use.

- The exact **amount of money you are suing for.**

- A **short summary of your case against the landlord –** *including dates and times of correspondence.*

Once the small claims clerk receives this information, **an officer of the court will serve your landlord with a notice that you have filed a lawsuit against him or her and that he or she must appear in court to put forth a defense.** Otherwise, *if the landlord fails to show up, the court will award a default judgment in your favor –* which you could use to collect the money to which you're entitled. **A judgment is simply the court's final decision that says you are entitled to whatever the court ordered.** And **judgments are easy to collect against landlords, unlike those awarded in other civil matters,** *because the landlord owns an investment property – which is very easy to put a lien on* should he or she fail to ever pay you. **A *lien* is a legal instrument used to file a claim against a property to ensure your judgment is satisfied.** If the landlord decides to refinance or sell the property, **you'll have to be paid before anything new can be financially finalized with the property.**

Chapter 12

How to Break a Lease: ...Without It Breaking You

This Chapter Discusses:

★ **What to Do**

★ **What Not to Do**

★ **Possible Consequences**

★ **Lawful Reasons**

I t's a fact of life for many **tenants that sign annual lease agreements**. You never know where life will take you one day to the next. So, if you've signed a long-term legally binding agreement to rent a place to live, **what can you do about it if you change your mind?** Unfortunately, *except in limited circumstances revealed later in this chapter, the decision is up to the landlord*, because that is to whom your lease agreement is pledged.

Remember the earlier references in this book pertaining to keeping your cool and not rocking the boat with your landlord unnecessarily? Well, **this is where that well-nurtured landlord-tenant relationship comes into play** – because if you've caused your landlord excessive amounts of grief without just cause, good luck on trying to get your landlord to bend the rules when he or she has got a signed contract from you.

Everything U Need to Know...

What to Do

Chances are your lease agreement will not have an early-release clause – so if you find out that you need to move (or that you just want to), **you have to handle this situation carefully.** *And the best way to do that is to be honest with your landlord.* Landlords (as well as others who deal with the general public on a regular basis) have a pretty good ability of reading someone. First of all, **if your reason for wanting to move is because of the condition of the rental or an issue with some of the amenities, contact the landlord over the phone or in person and express your concern and reservations about continuing to stay.** This is *not* the time to make a threat – only to express your concern and note ow unhappy you are. Granted, there are landlords that really don't care, but that's fortunately not the majority.

Landlords want nothing more than for you to pay the rent on time, take care of their property and treat them with respect. For reasons that are beyond the rental itself and apply to circumstances that are beyond your control, *you must let your landlord know as soon as possible that you may have to break your lease early.* This way, **you'll have a little more time to discuss reasonable remedies** and at least **give the landlord a head start on trying to find a replacement.**

Most states require landlords to make an earnest effort to fill a vacancy when a tenant breaks a lease as opposed to sitting idle for the remainder of your lease term. This may even be a good time to *offer to pitch in and help spread the word to find a replacement* and even offer to pay for an ad to run in a local newspaper or trade publication. Being the first to offer such a contribution (as opposed to being asked) just makes you look a whole lot better.

One of the most common ways for a landlord to allow you to break a lease **is if you find a new tenant *(sublessee)* to sublet your place for the remaining term of your lease.** This will *require your landlord's approval* – but as long as someone is there to keep the rent coming in each month, the landlord should have no complaints. Even if this wasn't addressed (or was prohibited) in the original lease agreement, **you and the landlord could always add a written addendum to now allow a sublease clause** that would be acknowledged by both of your signatures.

> **A word of caution about subletting:** If you sublet, *as the primary leaseholder you will still be responsible for future rent payments and property damage if the new tenant (sublessee) fails to pay rent or causes damage to the unit!* For these reasons, **it's always recommended to get the landlord to release you from your lease agreement, by having the new tenant become the leaseholder** – so that you're free and clear. However, either option would be acceptable.
>
> CAUTION

What Not to Do

When you need to break a lease, you never want to pack up your bags and leave in the middle of the night. *Nothing would make a landlord more upset than to discover that you've abandoned your unit and monthly rental obligations.* **Taking off without notice not only jeopardizes any legal grounds you may have had but can also lead to judgments and negative reporting on your consumer credit file** for the whole world to see when you apply for future extensions of credit (e.g., mortgage, car loan – and even another place to rent).

Believe it or not, it's not all just about the landlord's loss of rent. **If you vacate your apartment, the law is *rarely* on your side – even if you've been paying your rent on time up until you leave.** There isn't a court in the land that will rule in your favor if your landlord wants to pursue the matter and seek a judgment against you.

The bottom line is that you never want to turn your back on your landlord. *The goal is to work out a deal so you can move, preserve your landlord-tenant relationship and protect your creditworthiness.* Oh, and to ideally feel good about the whole arrangement. That's also important. Running in the middle of the night is not the healthiest way of handling what is supposed to be a normal situation. Rarely – if ever – should a night flight be necessary.

Possible Consequences

If you vacate without having an early-release clause in your lease agreement or your landlord's written permission, you could be in for a big surprise. Because, *in addition to being responsible for your monthly rent, you might have to pay for advertising, cleaning and other costs incurred by your landlord to fill your vacancy.* **So this could prove to be a very costly mistake on your part that could end up haunting you for years to come if your landlord decides to offer no mercy and take you to court.** Civil judgments *can remain on your credit file for at least seven years* for future landlords and creditors to see when you apply for a place to live or some other extension of credit.

Just remember – **when you break a lease without having a legitimate reason in the in the eyes of the law, every court in the land will side with the landlord.** So, if you feel you have a good case against your landlord as opposed to a mere desire to relocate or pursue better employment opportunities or whatever, **be sure you make every attempt to either communicate with your landlord or explore all available legal remedies** – including even **finding a local mediator** to assist in trying to resolve the problem. A *mediator* is **a person whose function is to assist both sides in finding an appropriate resolution.** Fortunately, **mediators for housing disputes are often government-subsidized and available free or for a minimal cost.** To find out if such a person exists in your local area, you must **contact your city or county government housing departments.**

If your dispute originates from your landlord not abiding by your lease agreement or violating state or local laws, try discussing the problem with him or her first. If this ends in a standoff, *then mail a certified letter to your landlord stating your intention to either contact the applicable authorities* (e.g., health department, building inspector, code enforcement) *or file a lawsuit in small claims court.* The great thing about **local authorities is that they can take action against your landlord**, *so you don't have to break your lease.* They will launch their own investigation – and **as long as they determine the landlord provided uninhabitable conditions, you are free to leave** without enduring the negative consequence typically associated with breaking a lease.

Lawful Reasons

There are essentially **three reasons that allow one to lawfully break a lease without being penalized.** The **first two**, however, **are subject to scrutiny and interpretation** – so you may want to seek professional legal advice or at least contact your local housing authorities before you act on this advice. *The third reason is clear-cut and cannot be challenged.*

Three Reasons to Legally Break a Lease:

☆ Health and Safety Are at Risk

If the landlord fails to repair problems that affect your health and safety after you've followed the appropriate notice provisions outlined in state or local laws, you may exercise your right to terminate your lease agreement. However, *this still doesn't mean you can leave in the middle of the night without giving notice to your landlord.* You will **always have to notify your landlord in advance of your intentions to vacate early** because of his or her violations. The amount of time required in advance will vary depending on your housing laws.

☆ Lack of Security

This reason is a little more difficult to prove. **In this particular instance, you must be able to show that the landlord has a blatant disregard for your security.** Now *this doesn't mean that if a criminal act is committed on the premises, you have the right to leave all of a sudden.* After all, a landlord cannot guarantee that no crime will ever occur. However, **a landlord is required to take reasonable measures to secure the property as defined by your state or local housing laws.** In other words, if you have repeatedly notified your landlord (preferably in writing) about missing or broken locking mechanisms on doors and windows and he or she fails to respond, most jurisdictions will be on your side. **Most landlords**

(unless they're slumlords) realize it's in their best interest to secure the property and limit their liability. Because *if something does happen to you after you've alerted them to the security problems, you (or your family) can sue them for failing to take corrective measures.*

★ Active Military Duty

You may terminate your lease agreement if you enlist, are drafted or are commissioned into active service in the U.S. Armed Forces or are a member of the Armed Forces or reserves called to active duty. In order to qualify, *you must be given orders to either permanently leave the area or relocate for at least 90 days.*

This also applies to a spouse or dependent, upon application to a court, under certain circumstances. This reason *does not apply if you knew about the change of duty station or retirement prior to signing the lease* – or knew that your term of enlistment would expire prior to the end of your lease term; it also *does not cover any residents* (other than your spouse or dependents) *who may be living on the premises with you.*

Chapter 13

Eviction:
Knowing When to Hold 'Em or Fold 'Em

This Chapter Discusses:

★ **What Is an Eviction?**

★ **The Eviction Process**

★ **How to Defend Against an Eviction**

★ **Options after the Verdict**

While the primary focus of this book is to empower you – the tenant – with the necessary information to protect your rights as a renter, **as you would expect, landlords also have rights and an expensive piece of investment they need to protect.** *Fortunately, landlords cannot legally take matters into their own hands and enforce their rights through coercion or retaliatory acts.* The **only remedy a landlord has for enforcing his or her rights** if you fail to comply with the terms of the lease agreement is to rely upon the law and **evict you from the premises.**

What Is an Eviction?

An *eviction* refers to **a lawsuit filed by a landlord to remove a tenant and his or her belongings from the landlord's property.** In most states, this is referred to as an *"unlawful detainer" lawsuit.* There are **thousands filed every day** in courts around the United States.

A landlord has a right to evict you for a number of reasons. The main reason is *for nonpayment of rent.* Other reasons include *when a tenant stays past the end of a lease term without renewing* (referred to as *"holding over"*), *engages in illegal activity from the premises* or *repeatedly violates other lease agreement terms.*

A landlord can refuse to renew a lease for any reason and can evict you as long as the landlord's reason is not considered an act of discrimination or retaliation against the tenant.

The Eviction Process

Forcibly removing a tenant from a rental property is not a simple or fast process. Some jurisdictions *may take more than a month for a landlord to have a tenant evicted.* Each of the **most common steps** is **outlined in this section, so you have a basic understanding of what to expect...**

Common Steps of the Eviction Process:

☆ Step 1: Notice to Vacate

The first step a landlord must take is **to terminate your tenancy by providing you with a formal** *notice to vacate.* This notice will inform you that *the landlord has terminated your tenancy and now requests you to vacate by a specific date or he or she will have you forcibly removed from the premises.*

At this point, no legal action has been filed in a court. Therefore, **unless you have a defense to present to fight the eviction** (discussed in the *next section* of the chapter), **now would be the best time to leave, so that there is no mention of this problem in the public record for other landlords to see.**

Note: *If the only reason the landlord is evicting you is because you failed to pay your rent, then this step will involve a notice to pay or quit instead.* The remedy for this situation is easy: **pay your past due rent!**

★ Step 2: Unlawful Detainer Lawsuit

If you fail to leave the premises or cure your late rent by the date specified in the notice, **the landlord must then file an *unlawful detainer lawsuit*.** Once this happens, **an officer of the court** (or sheriff) **will serve you with copies of the filing.** If you cannot be reached, the papers will be *posted in a visible location on the outside of the property* and a copy will simply be sent to you through the **U.S. Postal Service.**

Don't waste any effort trying to avoid being served – because it will not significantly delay the process, unlike other civil matters. **In fact, if you happen to have a defense, you might miss the opportunity to dispute the landlord's claims,** *resulting in you losing the case automatically.*

At this point, you really shouldn't be in the property – unless you have a defense or perhaps no place to go. **You will need to make a decision about whether or not you want to fight the eviction suit.** As soon as the landlord files an **unlawful detainer lawsuit**, it becomes *a permanent court record* and will become *accessible to any landlord that screens you for a future lease agreement.*

If you do choose to fight an eviction, be aware that you may be responsible for court costs *and the landlord's attorney fees* (if applicable and allowable under the law).

★ Step 3: Answering the Lawsuit

Once you receive a copy of the **lawsuit papers,** *make sure you read them carefully.* Included among them will be **a citation signed by the court clerk that will tell you the date and time you must appear for the hearing.** Generally, *you will have six to ten days to answer the eviction suit* after you've been served with the papers. **If you do not appear for the hearing, the court will automatically rule in the landlord's favor and award a default judgment against you.**

★ Step 4: The Hearing

At the hearing, you will need to be prepared to present your side of the story. *Take your copy of the lease agreement and any pictures, letters, documents, receipts or witnesses to present to the judge as evidence.* **Letters and even signed affidavits from witnesses will probably not be considered by the judge.** *You'll need to bring live persons with you if you want the court to hear their testimony.* If you need to, you can always request the clerk of the court to issue a subpoena to compel reluctant witnesses to show up and testify.

At the end of the hearing, the losing side will usually have the right to file an appeal in an attempt to get the court's decision overturned (reversed). *Appeals must be filed within a few days (usually five days) after the eviction proceedings have ended.*

How to Defend Against an Eviction

Once you receive the notice to vacate your residence and even before you receive the notice from the constable for your court hearing, **you should seriously consider whether you have any defenses available to the eviction suit.** As mentioned, in a nonpayment of rent eviction case, the only way to redeem yourself is to pay the past due rent. *Most courts will not consider cases of hardship (e.g., unemployment, illness, auto repairs).*

However, if you are in a **government-subsidized housing program such as Section 8,** *you should call your local legal aid organization because there are many more defenses available* (i.e., you may have a defense to nonpayment of rent if your public housing authority did not reduce your portion of rent after losing your job).

Defenses will be either *procedural* (i.e., the eviction suit was improperly brought before the court) **or** *substantive* (the landlord's case is invalid because you haven't violated any of the terms contained within the lease agreement).

Procedural defenses, while effective, **only end up stalling the eviction process. Even though the case will be dismissed on a technicality,** *dismissal does not prevent the landlord from correcting the mistake and then filing another lawsuit.* Procedural defenses will allow you more time either to settle with your landlord, to prepare a better defense or to find a new place to live.

★ Examples of Procedural Defenses Include:

- Lawsuit was **filed too early.**

- **Notice to vacate** (or pay or quit) **is unclear.**

- Notice to vacate was **delivered improperly** (e.g., left on front door step).

♦ Notice to vacate was **issued too early.**

♦ **Tenant was never given opportunity to cure (correct).**

Substantive defenses are truly case breakers, but are also terribly involved. *Allegations such as landlord retaliatory actions or discrimination* are difficult to prove and *will often require substantial evidence and witness testimony to convince the court.* These cases **will most certainly prompt the landlord** (if he or she loses) **to file a quick appeal in an attempt to protect his or her good name and to take the matter one step further. So, while very effective and longer lasting than a procedural defense,** *more time and effort will most certainly be involved.*

⭐ **Examples of Substantive Defenses Include:**

♦ **Retaliation**

♦ **Discrimination**

♦ **Uninhabitable living conditions**

♦ **Repairs or maintenance not performed**

♦ **Health, safety or security negligence**

Options after the Verdict

If the court rules against you, you'll have three options to choose from to put this part of your life to rest.

Three Options for a Tenant after Losing an Eviction Case:

★ Move Out

Just because you lost your case doesn't mean you shouldn't follow your normal vacating procedures. If you choose to move out, *don't leave any of your personal property behind.* **Be sure you clean the unit and perform an inspection of the property and document its condition with a camera or camcorder.** The last thing you need is to have your landlord accuse you of damaging the unit or appliances. And finally, *give a forwarding address to the landlord.*

★ Appeal

As mentioned before, **you will have a brief window of time to file an appeal.** If you really feel you've been ruled against unjustly and **want to appeal the court's eviction ruling,** *it would be in your best interest to consult a private attorney or a legal aid attorney* if you're a lower income tenant.

Typically, you'll have **five days** *(not just business days)* **to file an appeal.** Depending on the requirements of the court, *you may be asked to post an appeal bond guaranteeing a certain amount of money to be paid* (ultimately to the landlord), because you will cause the landlord to forgo collecting *any* rent for an additional period of time.

If you win your case and posted a cash bond, your money will be returned to you. *If you lose, the money will be used to pay court costs, the landlord's attorney fees and the landlord.* **Any remaining funds will then be returned to you.**

★ Do Nothing and Be Forcibly Removed

If you choose not to move out or appeal, the landlord will request a **Writ of Possession (a court order directing the sheriff to give back to the landlord rightful possession of the rental property)**.

The writ cannot be issued until at least five days (or whatever the appeal time frame may be) **after the court issues a judgment from the eviction hearing.** Upon being notified about the **Writ of Possession**, the sheriff will post *a 24-hour notice on the rental property's door,* instructing you that **the sheriff will be back to remove you and any other remaining occupants from the property.** *This will also include all of your personal possessions.*

At anytime during the eviction process (although rare), **you can try negotiating with your landlord to settle any past due rent or legal fees – *but don't count on it.* Not many landlords are willing to take another chance on someone who has caused them this much grief.**

However, if the landlord seems to be receptive to an offer, make sure you get it in writing. **There are a few landlords out there that will try to grab a little more money from you and then still proceed with the eviction.** Unfortunately, there's very little room for oral agreements in today's society…

Chapter 14

Becoming a Homeowner: Renting Vs. Owning

This Chapter Discusses:

★ **Qualifying for a Mortgage Loan**
★ **Leasing with an Option to Buy**
★ **How to Shop for a Home**

The choice is yours: **Do you want to rent for the rest of your life or do you want to own your own home?** It's really a matter of personal preference – because you can choose to do either, **each with its individual pros and cons.** Maybe not at this very moment, but – with a little planning and effort – anyone can own a home. This final chapter is **intended to benefit those who may think homeownership is unattainable.** *Quite the contrary, it's actually not that difficult.* While this chapter will introduce the basic concepts of buying a home, an entire volume is available from the **"EUNTK" series**, titled *American Home Buying*, for when you actually become serious about buying as opposed to renting. For now, **here's the lowdown on becoming a homeowner…**

Qualifying for a Mortgage Loan

Without giving you an entire lesson on the properties of a **mortgage**, just **think of it as a car loan – except that a mortgage loan is used for a house.** This is the reason why most renters don't seriously consider homeownership as an option. They don't think they can qualify or afford the monthly mortgage payment. But don't sweat it – **getting approved for a few hundred thousand dollars is not that big a deal –** *really.* There are **three steps involved in qualifying for a mortgage** and they are explained as follows:

Three Requirements That Must Be Met to Qualify for a Mortgage:

★ Credit

You need credit to get credit and a mortgage is the single largest extension of credit that you will most likely ever apply for in your life. So the first step involves *getting your credit report into shape.*

As you probably already know, there are **three main credit bureaus** that provide credit reports: **Equifax, Experian** and **TransUnion.** Traditional mortgage lenders like to see *at least two of these credit reports with a credit score of 620 or above* to consider you for a mortgage loan. (There is a **different group of mortgage lenders that may entertain a lower score,** but these are considered nonprime lenders and are not discussed in this volume, due to their **unfavorable financing terms.**)

In addition to having at least two credit scores of 620 or above, **you will also need at least three open accounts** (e.g., **credit cards, car loans, student loans**, etc.). Most lenders will consider a recently closed account as an open account as long as it was closed within the past 12 months. However, **lenders will each have their own set of guidelines and requirements that can change at anytime throughout the year.**

Employment

Believe it or not, **the ability to afford a mortgage payment is not the issue** – since **there are plenty of programs offered to allow you to afford almost any payment within reason** *(your housing payment should not exceed 50% of your income, preferably 42%).*

Most lenders simply want you to be able to **verify that you've been steadily employed in the same line of work for the past two years.** *Working for different employers is not a problem, but if you completely change into an unrelated field* (i.e., working as a plumber and then an accountant), *this may present a problem that requires a good explanation.*

⭐ Savings

This is not about having to amass a large down payment, another common misconception. *There are plenty of $0 down mortgage loans and government assistance programs.* The main concern of most lenders is that **you have the equivalent of two months' worth of a mortgage payment to cover your principal, interest, taxes and insurance sitting in some type of bank account or brokerage account** [e.g., mutual funds, stocks, bonds, IRA, 401(k)].

This not only **demonstrates your ability to manage your money,** but **also provides a documented source of cash to continue making your mortgage payment if you should lose your job.** *Lenders are all about reducing their risk.* This is why riskier mortgage programs require as much as six months of reserves (even twelve months has been seen before). But don't worry – **most traditional mortgage programs just require two months.**

As one would expect, **there's obviously more involved in getting approved for the mortgage,** but **if you can meet these three basic requirements, your chances of an approval are very high.** The *best course of action* is to **contact a reputable lender** of your choice as far in advance as possible to ask exactly what the lender's requirements are – so *you can prepare for the application process by making sure you've saved enough, repaired your credit and assembled all of the necessary documents needed to approve you.*

For a more in-depth look at how to finance a home, check out the *American Mortgage* volume from **EUNTK** for **easy, step-by-step instructions.**

Leasing with an Option to Buy

If you determine that your situation requires a larger down payment or additional time (i.e., perhaps your credit needs a little extra work), *this is a lease addendum (called a "purchase option") that can be added to any residential lease agreement and is worth considering.* This is an **industry-accepted way** to purchase the very property that you are renting.

There Are Two Essential Ideas Behind the Purchase Option:

★ Predetermine the Purchase Price

Usually done at the time of the original lease signing, this addendum *gives you the right to purchase the property at a fixed price that was determined a year or two earlier*. This is a great deal if the property value increases – but **chances are a landlord would only consider discounting the sales price if the market has been either distressed or sluggish**.

★ Build a Down Payment

"Purchase options" can state that **a portion of the rent is to be credited toward the tenant's down payment**. In this case, **rent payments are usually adjusted upward,** *with at least 100% or more of the adjustment credited toward the down payment*. **In such an instance, this down payment credit is usually required by law** (check with your lender or even your state's equivalent to a banking and finance or real estate department) **to be kept in a separate escrow bank account,** *so the funds are not intermingled with your own personal funds* – thereby, clearly establishing the distinction of their intended use.

An example of how to build a down payment using an *option to purchase agreement* **appears below.**

Let's say the monthly rent is normally $1,050 – and the option states that you have the right to purchase your home at any time prior to January 1, 2010, for a purchase price of $150,000. The landlord would require an *initial, non-refundable* **"option payment"** of $2,000 *in lieu of a security deposit* – and, *along with the monthly rent*, **there would be an additional option payment of $250 per month.** Therefore, the **total monthly payment for you is $1,300** *($1,050 rent + $250 option to buy)*. **All of the option money paid is** *non-refundable*, but this takes the place of having to worry about the security deposit!

EXAMPLE

You can see the **advantage of this option**, where it **allows you time** (with terms of up to 24 months available) **to save up for the down payment** (and time to improve your credit, if needed), **while** – in the meantime – **the purchase price remains fixed**.

⭐ **A 24-month option on a home with a base rent of $1,050 per month and a $150,000 purchase price could be calculated like this:**

- ♦ **Option (in Lieu of a Security Deposit): $2,000**

- ♦ **Monthly Option Payment:** $250 @ 24 months = **$6,000**

- ♦ **Total Down Payment (Credit): $8,000** (non-refundable)

This **$8,000 can be applied to the purchase of the home** and *represents more than 5% of the purchase price of $150,000.* Depending on your credit, income and assets, **this amount is usually an acceptable down payment in most situations.** And, as far as the move-in expenses, **the cost of the option payment is about the same as moving into any other rental.**

☆ Move-in expenses for the tenant would be as follows:

- **First Month's Rent: $1,300 ($1,050 + $250 monthly option)**

- **Initial Option Fee: $2,000** (in lieu of a security deposit)

- **Total Move-In Expenses: $3,300**

A sample of an **"option to purchase"** agreement appears on the next page – and can also be found **on the enclosed CD-ROM.** However, it is *strongly suggested* that *both you and the landlord* **contact a licensed mortgage lender to find out exactly what the underwriting requirements are for such an agreement** – especially if you intend on using this method to build a down payment or a **"gift of equity."** The state of the mortgage industry has been in such turmoil of late that **lenders are continually modifying their loan product matrices, terms and conditions to reduce their foreclosure risk**, while – at the same time – trying to remain competitive enough to survive in the marketplace.

Option to Purchase Agreement

Instructions:
1. Insert your IMAGE or LOGO (optional)
2. Highlight & complete AGREEMENT FIELDS
3. REPLACE ALL of this text with YOUR contact info
4. Click on 'PRINT FORM' when finished

Everything U Need to Know...

Click here to insert image/logo

Option to Purchase Leased Property

OPTION TO PURCHASE

This agreement is entered into between _____, of
_____, _____, _____ County,
_____, referred to as "lessor," and _____, of
_____, _____, _____ County,
_____, referred to as "lessee."

Lessor agrees to sell to lessee, at their option, the following property owned by lessor, namely:
_____, _____, _____ County,
_____, subject to the following terms and conditions:

1. This option to purchase will expire on _____.

2. Notice of election to purchase by lessee shall be in writing and given to lessor by _____.

3. The price to be paid for the property, if this option is exercised, is $ _____ dollars.
After payment is made to lessor in full, lessor agrees to execute and deliver to lessee a deed conveying the
property to lessee, and to deliver possession of property free of all liens and encumbrances.

4. _____
_____

5. _____
_____

ORIGINAL LEASE AGREEMENT

All other terms and covenants of the original Lease Agreement shall remain in full force and effect.

In witness of the above, each party to this agreement has caused it to be executed on the date below.

Signature of lessor: _____ Date: _____

Signature of lessee: _____ Date: _____

Signature of lessee: _____ Date: _____

This form provided by USLandlord.com

SAMPLE

How to Shop for a Home

As soon as you determine you can qualify for a mortgage, **be sure that you first contact a lender to check exactly how much you can afford to spend** (typically this figure is *three times your household income*). Once you have that maximum purchase price in mind, it's time to go to the real estate mall and try on as many homes as possible!

This is when **it is strongly suggested** *(especially if you're a first time homebuyer!)* **that you contact a local real estate agent to represent you. Don't worry –** *it won't cost you a dime, because you are the buyer.* Buyers don't pay commission to real estate agents; only sellers do. So **at this point in time, it's worth having the free representation.** Real estate agents (at least the experienced ones) not only can **help you find a home,** but **also can help you negotiate the best deal** and **even handle all of the paperwork required to finalize the transaction.**

There's **much more than this chapter could possibly reveal about the mounds of paperwork to finance and close on a home** – so *it's important that you seek professional assistance.* If you prefer, **you can begin shopping on the Internet** (there are thousands of sites, but **Realtor.com** pretty much covers it all) **before you contact a real estate agent.**

It's strongly recommended that you contact an agent who is independent from the seller. While it's ethical and legal for a real estate agent to represent both the buyer and the seller, *it's better if you have someone sitting in your corner tending only to your needs* – as opposed to running back and forth across the ring, trying to satisfy both parties. However, **if your real estate agent happens to represent the seller on a property that you were shown, don't let this deter you from getting the home you want.**

So, there you have it... **Everything U Need to Know...** about your rights and responsibilities as an **American Tenant.** Ideally, you've found the information you sought to discover, as well as gained an understanding of the perspective from the American landlord.

We wish you the best of luck and hope **this volume has helped empower you with** ***the knowledge to succeed as an* American Tenant.** And while this volume can't possibly address *every situation,* it should have given you the overview you need and provided sufficient additional resources, which can steer you in the right direction...

If you ever need further advice or assistance, you can *always* **check out the official website for this entire book series** at **www.EUNTK.com** – where you'll find discussion groups, laws and statutes, other related subjects within the series and a whole lot more... Remember, **this site is free** – and you can't beat that ***for the absolute easiest way there is to learn*** "Everything U Need to Know..."

For additional information about **landlord-tenant laws,** please refer to the *American Landlord Law* volume available at book retailers nationwide.

Landlord-Tenant Laws:
A Summary of State Guidelines

This Appendix Includes:

- ★ **Returned Check Fees**
- ★ **Security Deposit Limits**
- ★ **Security Deposit Interest Requirements**
- ★ **Deadlines for Returning Security Deposits**
- ★ **Notice of Entry Requirements**
- ★ **Late Fees**

The guidelines contained in this appendix are provided to assist you in drafting and enforcing your lease agreement. While this information is deemed accurate, you are encouraged to **consult an expert in the area of landlord-tenant law** – or at least contact your state's equivalent of a **"department of real estate,"** to make sure the information provided in this appendix is still current at the time you are referencing it.

If you require a more comprehensive legal resource regarding your rights and responsibilities as an **American Tenant** (as opposed to a brief appendix on the subject), we recommend *American Landlord Law: Everything U Need to Know about Landlord-Tenant Laws* – available at book retailers nationwide or through **www.EverythingUNeedToKnow.com**. This essential companion explains in great detail *the most critical aspects of landlord-tenant law* in an easy-to-read format, so you will be able to understand all the fine details in order to adequately **protect yourself from the commonly encountered unforeseen legal pitfalls**.

Returned Check Fees

Alabama	$30 - Check writer is also responsible for all other costs of collection.
Alaska	$30
Arizona	$25
Arkansas	$25
California	$25
Colorado	$20 - Check writer is also responsible for all other costs of collection.
Connecticut	$20 - Check writer is also responsible for all other costs of collection.
Delaware	$40
District of Columbia	$25
Florida	Checks from (1) $0.01-$50.00 = $25.00 fee, (2) $50.01-$300.00 = $30.00 fee, (3) $300.01 and over = the greater of $40.00 fee or 5% of the face amount of the check. Check writer is also responsible for all other costs of Collection.
Georgia	$30 or 5% of the face amount of the check, whichever is greater.
Hawaii	$30 - Check writer is also responsible for all other costs of collection.
Idaho	$20 - Check writer is also responsible for all other costs of collection.
Illinois	$25 - Check writer is also responsible for all other costs of collection.
Indiana	$20 - Check writer is also responsible for all other costs of collection.
Iowa	$30
Kansas	$30
Kentucky	$25
Louisiana	$25 or 5% of the face amount of the check, whichever is greater.
Maine	$25
Maryland	$35
Massachusetts	$25
Michigan	$25
Minnesota	$30 - Check writer is also responsible for all other costs of collection and civil penalties may be imposed for nonpayment.

Mississippi	$40
Missouri	$25
Montana	$30
Nebraska	$35
Nevada	$25
New Hampshire	$25
New Jersey	$30
New Mexico	$30
New York	$20 - Check writer is also responsible for all other costs of collection.
North Carolina	$25
North Dakota	$30
Ohio	$30 or 10% of the face amount of the check, whichever is greater.
Oklahoma	$25
Oregon	$25
Pennsylvania	$30
Rhode Island	$25
South Carolina	$30
South Dakota	$40
Tennessee	$30 - Check writer is also responsible for all other costs of collection.
Texas	$30 - Other costs of collection may be charged.
Utah	$20 - Check writer is also responsible for all other costs of collection.
Vermont	$25
Virginia	$35
Washington	$30 - This amount is assessed as a Handling Fee for returned checks. Check writer is also responsible for all other costs of collection.
West Virginia	$25
Wisconsin	$20 - Check writer is also responsible for all other costs of collection.
Wyoming	$25 - Check writer is also responsible for all other costs of collection.

Security Deposit Limits

Alabama	1 month's rent
Alaska	2 months' rent, limit does not apply unless monthly rent exceeds $2,000
Arizona	1 ½ months' rent unless both parties agree to more
Arkansas	2 months' rent
California	2 months' rent if unfurnished unit; 3 months' rent if furnished unit; extra ½ month's rent if tenant has waterbed
Colorado	No statute
Connecticut	2 months' rent, 1 month's rent if tenant is 62 or older
Delaware	No limit if furnished unit or if month-to-month tenancy; 1 month's rent if year or longer lease
District of Columbia	1 month's rent
Florida	No statute
Georgia	No statute
Hawaii	1 month's rent
Idaho	No statute
Illinois	No statute
Indiana	No statute
Iowa	2 months' rent
Kansas	1 month's rent if unfurnished unit; 1 ½ months' rent if furnished unit
Kentucky	No statute
Louisiana	No statute
Maine	2 months' rent
Maryland	2 months' rent
Massachusetts	1 month's rent
Michigan	1 ½ months' rent
Minnesota	No statute
Mississippi	No statute

Missouri	2 months' rent
Montana	No statute
Nebraska	1 month's rent
Nevada	3 months' rent
New Hampshire	$100 or 1 month's rent, whichever greater; no limit if landlord and tenant share facilities
New Jersey	1 ½ months' rent
New Mexico	1 month's rent if less than 1-year lease; no limit if year or longer lease
New York	No limit unless covered by local rent control regulations
North Carolina	1 ½ months' rent if month-to-month tenancy; 2 months' rent if lease term longer than 2 months
North Dakota	1 month's rent
Ohio	No statute
Oklahoma	No statute
Oregon	No statute
Pennsylvania	2 months' rent first year of tenancy; 1 month's rent all future years
Rhode Island	1 month's rent
South Carolina	No statute
South Dakota	1 month's rent
Tennessee	No statute
Texas	No statute
Utah	No statute
Vermont	No statute
Virginia	2 months' rent
Washington	No statute
West Virginia	No statute
Wisconsin	No statute
Wyoming	No statute

Security Deposit Interest Requirements

Alabama	No statute
Alaska	No statute
Arizona	No statute
Arkansas	No statute
California	No statute
Colorado	No statute
Connecticut	Pay annually and at termination, equal to average rate on savings accts at insured banks but not less than 1.5%
Delaware	No statute
District of Columbia	Pay at termination, at current passbook rate
Florida	Not required, but if made must pay annually and at termination; tenant who wrongfully terminates is not entitled to; lease agreement must give details on interest
Georgia	No statute
Hawaii	No statute
Idaho	No statute
Illinois	Required if owner has 25+ properties adjacent to each other or in same building; if security deposit held for longer than 6 months, must pay annually and at termination
Indiana	No statute
Iowa	Not required, but if paid must pay at termination; however, any interest earned during the first 5 years is landlord's
Kansas	No statute
Kentucky	No statute
Louisiana	No statute
Maine	No statute
Maryland	Must pay semi-annually, at a rate of 4% if deposit is greater than $50
Massachusetts	Must pay annually and within 30 days of termination, at a rate of 5% or the actual rate earned; no interest for last month's rent paid in advance
Michigan	No statute

Minnesota	Must pay at a rate of 1%; total interest under $1 does not need to be paid
Mississippi	No statute
Missouri	No statute
Montana	No statute
Nebraska	No statute
Nevada	No statute
New Hampshire	Only required if deposit held for a year or longer; must pay at termination; tenant can request payment every 3 years if request made within 30 days of tenancy expiration/renewal; rate must be equal to the rate paid on the bank savings account where deposited
New Jersey	Must pay annually or credit back to rent owed; landlord with less than 10 units can put deposit in any insured interest-bearing bank account; those with 10 or more must put funds in an insured money market account that matures in a year or less or in any other account that pays interest at a comparable rate to a money market account
New Mexico	Must pay annually at rate equal to passbook rate if deposit is more than 1 month's rent and there is a year lease
New York	Must pay at prevailing rate if unit is covered under rent control or stabilization requirements or if building has 6 or more units; landlord can keep 1% admin fee a year
North Carolina	No statute
North Dakota	Must pay interest if tenancy is at least 9 months; deposit must be put in an insured interest-bearing savings or checking acct
Ohio	Must pay annually and at termination, at a rate of 5% if the tenancy is 6 months or more and the deposit is greater than $50 or 1 month's rent - whichever is greater - the interest only accrues on the excess of the $50 or 1-month-rent amount
Oklahoma	No statute
Oregon	No statute
Pennsylvania	Must pay if tenancy is longer than 2 years; interest accrues from start of 25th month of tenancy and must be paid annually after that point; landlord can deduct 1% fee
Rhode Island	No statute
South Carolina	No statute
South Dakota	No statute
Tennessee	No statute

Texas	No statute
Utah	No statute
Vermont	No statute
Virginia	Must pay if deposit is held for more than 13 months for continued tenancy in same unit; interest accrues from start of lease and must be paid at termination; must be at rate of 1% below FED discount rate as of Jan. 1 of each year
Washington	No statute
West Virginia	No statute
Wisconsin	No statute
Wyoming	No statute

Deadlines for Returning Security Deposits

Alabama	35 days
Alaska	14 days if proper termination notice given; 30 days if not
Arizona	14 days
Arkansas	30 days
California	21 days
Colorado	1 month unless lease provides for longer period up to 60 days; 72 weekday non-holiday hours if emergency termination due to gas equipment hazard
Connecticut	30 days or within 15 days of receipt of forwarding address from tenant, whichever is later
Delaware	20 days
District of Columbia	45 days
Florida	15 days if no deductions; 30 days to give notice of what deductions will be made; then tenant has 15 days to dispute any deduction and remaining deposit must be returned within 30 days of initial deduction notification
Georgia	1 month
Hawaii	14 days
Idaho	21 days unless both parties agree; then up to 30 days
Illinois	45 days if no deductions; 30 days to itemize deductions
Indiana	45 days
Iowa	30 days
Kansas	30 days
Kentucky	No statute deadline for returning; if the tenant leaves owing the last month's rent and does not request their security deposit back, the landlord may apply the security deposit to the rent owed after 30 days; if the tenant leaves owing no rent and having a refund due to them, the landlord must send an itemization to the tenant; but if the tenant does not respond to the landlord after 60 days, the landlord may keep the deposit
Louisiana	1 month
Maine	21 days if tenancy at will; 30 days if written lease
Maryland	45 days; 10 days to itemize deductions if tenant utilizes a surety bond
Massachusetts	30 days

Michigan	30 days
Minnesota	3 weeks; 5 days if termination due to condemnation
Mississippi	45 days
Missouri	30 days
Montana	10 days if no deductions; 30 days if deductions
Nebraska	14 days
Nevada	30 days
New Hampshire	30 days; if shared facilities and deposit is more than 30 days' rent, then 20 days unless written agreement otherwise
New Jersey	30 days; 5 days if termination due to fire, flood, condemnation, evacuation; deadline does not apply if property is owner-occupied and has only 1 or 2 units if the tenant did not provide a written 30 days notification to the landlord of their desire to invoke the law
New Mexico	30 days
New York	Reasonable time
North Carolina	30 days
North Dakota	30 days
Ohio	30 days
Oklahoma	30 days
Oregon	31 days
Pennsylvania	30 days
Rhode Island	20 days
South Carolina	30 days
South Dakota	2 weeks to return deposit and/or provide explanation for any withholding; 45 days to provide an itemized accounting of all deductions made to the security deposit if the tenant requests one
Tennessee	No statute; 10 days to itemize deductions
Texas	30 days
Utah	30 days or within 15 days of receipt of forwarding address from tenant, whichever is later
Vermont	14 days

Virginia	45 days
Washington	14 days
West Virginia	No statute
Wisconsin	21 days
Wyoming	30 days or within 15 days of receipt of forwarding address from tenant, whichever is later; 60 days if unit has damage

Notice of Entry Requirements

Alabama	2 days
Alaska	24 hours
Arizona	2 days
Arkansas	Not specified
California	24 hours; 48 hours if preliminary inspection
Colorado	No statute
Connecticut	Reasonable time
Delaware	2 days
District of Columbia	No statute
Florida	12 hours
Georgia	No statute
Hawaii	2 days
Idaho	No statute
Illinois	No statute
Indiana	Reasonable time
Iowa	24 hours
Kansas	Reasonable time
Kentucky	2 days
Louisiana	No statute
Maine	24 hours
Maryland	No statute
Massachusetts	Not specified
Michigan	No statute
Minnesota	Reasonable time
Mississippi	No statute
Missouri	No statute

Montana	24 hours
Nebraska	1 day
Nevada	24 hours
New Hampshire	Adequate notice for the circumstance
New Jersey	No statute
New Mexico	24 hours
New York	No statute
North Carolina	No statute
North Dakota	Reasonable time
Ohio	24 hours
Oklahoma	1 day
Oregon	24 hours
Pennsylvania	No statute
Rhode Island	2 days
South Carolina	24 hours
South Dakota	No statute
Tennessee	Not specified
Texas	No statute
Utah	Not specified
Vermont	24 hours
Virginia	24 hours
Washington	2 days
West Virginia	No statute
Wisconsin	Advanced notice, unless lease provides time frame
Wyoming	No statute

Late Fees

Alabama	No statute
Alaska	No statute
Arizona	Late fees must be reasonable and indicated in the lease agreement.
Arkansas	No statute
California	Late fees must be close to the landlord's actual losses and indicated in the lease agreement as follows: "Because landlord and tenant agree that actual damages for late rent payments are very difficult or impossible to determine, landlord and tenant agree to the following stated late charge as liquidated damages."
Colorado	No statute
Connecticut	Late fees can be charged when rent is 9 days late.
Delaware	Late fees cannot be more than 5% of the rent amount due and can be charged when the rent is more than 5 days late. If the landlord does not have an office within the rental property's county, the tenant has an additional 3 days before late fees can be charged.
District of Columbia	No statute
Florida	No statute
Georgia	No statute
Hawaii	No statute
Idaho	No statute
Illinois	No statute
Indiana	No statute
Iowa	Late fees cannot be more than $10 a day with a maximum of $40 a month allowed.
Kansas	No statute
Kentucky	No statute
Louisiana	No statute
Maine	Late fees cannot be more than 4% of the rent amount due for a 30-day period and must be indicated in writing to the tenant at the start of their tenancy. Late fees can be charged when rent is 15 days late.
Maryland	Late fees cannot be more than 5% of the rent amount due.

Massachusetts	Late fees can be charged when rent is 30 days late.
Michigan	No statute
Minnesota	No statute
Mississippi	No statute
Missouri	No staute
Montana	No statute
Nebraska	No statute
Nevada	Late fees must be indicated in the lease agreement.
New Hampshire	No statute
New Jersey	Late fees can be charged when rent is 5 days late.
New Mexico	Late fees cannot be more than 10% of the rent amount due per rental period. Tenant must be notified of the late fee charged by the end of the next rental period.
New York	No statute
North Carolina	Late fees cannot be more than 5% of the rent amount due or $15, whichever is greater, and can be charged when rent is 5 days late.
North Dakota	No statute
Ohio	No statute
Oklahoma	No statute
Oregon	Late fees cannot be more than a reasonable amount charged by others in the same market if a flat fee is utilized; if a daily charge is utilized, it cannot be more than 6% of the reasonable flat fee with a maximum of 5% of the rent amount due per rental period allowed. Late fees can be charged when rent is 4 days late and must be indicated in the lease agreement.
Pennsylvania	No statute
Rhode Island	No statute
South Carolina	No statute
South Dakota	No statute
Tennessee	Late fees can be charged when rent is 5 days late and cannot be more than 10% of the late rent amount. However, if the fifth day is a weekend or holiday and the tenant pays the rent amount due on the following business day, a late fee cannot be charged.

Texas	Late fees must be reasonable and close to the landlord's actual losses. Late fees must be indicted in the lease agreement and can be charged when the rent is 2 days late. Late fees can include an initial fee as well as a daily fee for each day the rent is late thereafter.
Utah	No statute
Vermont	No statute
Virginia	No statute
Washington	No statute
West Virginia	No statute
Wisconsin	No statute
Wyoming	No statute

Government Forms and Publications:
Landlord Responsibilities

This Appendix Includes:

★ **Are You a Victim of Housing Discrimination?**

★ **Fair Housing: Equal Opportunity for All**

★ **Lead-Based Paint Pamphlet**

★ **Lead-Based Paint Disclosure**

★ **FCRA Summary of Rights**

The following forms and publications were produced by the **Department of Housing and Urban Development** and the **Federal Trade Commission** for your use as an **American Tenant**. Unlike many of the government forms that can be easily tossed aside and ignored, *these documents are actually worth examining* – if for no reason other than to educate yourself... *especially* if you plan on renting in some of the older homes around town that were constructed prior to 1978.

Remember – required disclosures should *always* be examined *prior to using them*. **Never** take your rights and responsibilities as an **American Tenant** for granted.

Are You a Victim of Housing Discrimination?

Are You a

Victim of

Housing

Discrimination?

Fair Housing is Your Right!

If you have been denied your housing rights...you may have experienced unlawful discrimination.

U.S. Department of Housing and Urban Development

WHERE TO MAIL YOUR FORM OR INQUIRE ABOUT YOUR CLAIM

For Connecticut, Maine, Massachusetts, New Hampshire, Rhode Island, and Vermont:
NEW ENGLAND OFFICE
Fair Housing Hub
U.S. Dept. of Housing and Urban Development
Thomas P. O'Neill, Jr. Federal Building
10 Causeway Street, Room 321
Boston, MA 02222-1092
Telephone (617) 994-8320 or 1-800-827-5005
Fax (617) 565-7313 • TTY (617) 565-5453
E-mail: **Complaints_office_01@hud.gov**

For New Jersey and New York:
NEW YORK/NEW JERSEY OFFICE
Fair Housing Hub
U.S. Dept. of Housing and Urban Development
26 Federal Plaza, Room 3532
New York, NY 10278-0068
Telephone (212) 264-1290 or 1-800-496-4294
Fax (212) 264-9829 • TTY (212) 264-0927
E-mail: **Complaints_office_02@hud.gov**

For Delaware, District of Columbia, Maryland, Pennsylvania, Virginia, and West Virginia:
MID-ATLANTIC OFFICE
Fair Housing Hub
U.S. Dept. of Housing and Urban Development
The Wanamaker Building
100 Penn Square East
Philadelphia, PA 19107
Telephone (215) 656-0663 or 1-888-799-2085
Fax (215) 656-3419 • TTY (215) 656-3450
E-mail: **Complaints_office_03@hud.gov**

For Alabama, the Caribbean, Florida, Georgia, Kentucky, Mississippi, North Carolina, South Carolina, and Tennessee:
SOUTHEAST/CARIBBEAN OFFICE
Fair Housing Hub
U.S. Dept. of Housing and Urban Development
Five Points Plaza
40 Marietta Street, 16th Floor
Atlanta, GA 30303-2808
Telephone (404) 331-5140 or 1-800-440-8091
Fax (404) 331-1021 • TTY (404) 730-2654
E-mail: **Complaints_office_04@hud.gov**

For Illinois, Indiana, Michigan, Minnesota, Ohio, and Wisconsin:
MIDWEST OFFICE
Fair Housing Hub
U.S. Dept. of Housing and Urban Development
Ralph H. Metcalfe Federal Building
77 West Jackson Boulevard, Room 2101
Chicago, IL 60604-3507
Telephone (312) 353-7776 or 1-800-765-9372
Fax (312) 886-2837 • TTY (312) 353-7143
E-mail: **Complaints_office_05@hud.gov**

For Arkansas, Louisiana, New Mexico, Oklahoma, and Texas:
SOUTHWEST OFFICE
Fair Housing Hub
U.S. Dept. of Housing and Urban Development
801 North Cherry, 27th Floor
Fort Worth, TX 76102
Telephone (817) 978-5900 or 1-888-560-8913
Fax (817) 978-5876 or 5851 • TTY (817) 978-5595
E-mail: **Complaints_office_06@hud.gov**

For Iowa, Kansas, Missouri and Nebraska:
GREAT PLAINS OFFICE
Fair Housing Hub
U.S. Dept. of Housing and Urban Development
Gateway Tower II
400 State Avenue, Room 200, 4th Floor
Kansas City, KS 66101-2406
Telephone (913) 551-6958 or 1-800-743-5323
Fax (913) 551-6856 • TTY (913) 551-6972
E-mail: **Complaints_office_07@hud.gov**

For Colorado, Montana, North Dakota, South Dakota, Utah, and Wyoming:
ROCKY MOUNTAINS OFFICE
Fair Housing Hub
U.S. Dept. of Housing and Urban Development
1670 Broadway
Denver, CO 80202-4801
Telephone (303) 672-5437 or 1-800-877-7353
Fax (303) 672-5026 • TTY (303) 672-5248
E-mail: **Complaints_office_08@hud.gov**

For Arizona, California, Hawaii, and Nevada:
PACIFIC/HAWAII OFFICE
Fair Housing Hub
U.S. Dept. of Housing and Urban Development
600 Harrison Street, Third Floor
San Francisco, CA 94107-1300
Telephone (415) 489-6524 or 1-800-347-3739
Fax (415) 489-6558 • TTY (415) 436-6594
E-mail: **Complaints_office_09@hud.gov**

For Alaska, Idaho, Oregon, and Washington:
NORTHWEST/ALASKA OFFICE
Fair Housing Hub
U.S. Dept. of Housing and Urban Development
Seattle Federal Office Building
909 First Avenue, Room 205
Seattle, WA 98104-1000
Telephone (206) 220-5170 or 1-800-877-0246
Fax (206) 220-5447 • TTY (206) 220-5185
E-mail: **Complaints_office_10@hud.gov**

If after contacting the local office nearest you, you still have questions – you may contact HUD further at:
U.S. Dept. of Housing and Urban Development
Office of Fair Housing and Equal Opportunity
451 7th Street, S.W., Room 5204
Washington, DC 20410-2000
Telephone (202) 708-0836 or 1-800-669-9777
Fax (202) 708-1425 • TTY 1-800-927-9275

To file electronically, visit: www.hud.gov

```
_____
_____
_____
_____
```

PLACE
POSTAGE
HERE

MAIL TO:

```
_____
_____
_____
_____
```

Public Reporting Burden for this collection of information is estimated to average 20 minutes per response, including the time for reviewing instructions, searching existing data sources, gathering and maintaining the data needed, and completing and reviewing the collection of information.

The Department of Housing and Urban Development is authorized to collect this information by Title VIII of the Civil Rights Act of 1968, as amended by the Fair Housing Amendments Act of 1988, (P.L. 100-430); Title VI of the Civil Rights Act of 1964, (P.L. 88-352); Section 504 of the Rehabilitation Act of 1973, as amended, (P.L. 93-112); Section 109 of Title I- Housing and Community Development Act of 1974, as amended, (P.L. 97-35); Americans with Disabilities Act of 1990, (P.L. 101-336); and by the Age Discrimination Act of 1975, as amended, (42 U.S.C. 6103).

The information will be used to investigate and to process housing discrimination complaints. The information may be disclosed to the United States Department of Justice for its use in the filing of pattern and practice suits of housing discrimination or the prosecution of the person(s) who committed that discrimination where violence is involved; and to State or local fair housing agencies that administer substantially equivalent fair housing laws for complaint processing. Failure to provide some or all of the requested information will result in delay or denial of HUD assistance.

Disclosure of this information is voluntary.

HOUSING DISCRIMINATION INFORMATION

Departamento de Vivienda y Desarrollo Urbano   Oficina de Derecho Equitativo a la Vivienda
U.S. Department of Housing and Urban Development   Office of Fair Housing and Equal Opportunity

Instructions: (Please type or print) Read this form carefully. Try to answer all questions. If you do not know the answer or a question does not apply to you, leave the space blank. You have one year from the date of the alleged discrimination to file a complaint. Your form should be signed and dated.

Your Name

Your Address

City   State   Zip Code

Best time to call   Your Daytime Phone No   Evening Phone No

Who else can we call if we cannot reach you?

Contact's Name   Best Time to call

Daytime Phone No   Evening Phone No

Contact's Name   Best Time to call

Daytime Phone No   Evening Phone No

1 What happened to you?
How were you discriminated against?
For example: were you refused an opportunity to rent or buy housing? Denied a loan? Told that housing was not available when in fact it was? Treated differently from others seeking housing?
State briefly what happened.

Form HUD-903.1 (1/02)   OMB Approval No. 2529-0011 (exp. 1/31/2011)

HOUSING DISCRIMINATION INFORMATION

Departamento de Vivienda y Desarrollo Urbano   Oficina de Derecho Equitativo a la Vivienda
U.S. Department of Housing and Urban Development   Office of Fair Housing and Equal Opportunity

2 Why do you think you are a victim of housing discrimination?

Is it because of your:

· race · color · religion · sex · national origin · familial status (families with children under 18) · disability?

For example: were you denied housing because of your race? Were you denied a mortgage loan because of your religion? Or turned down for an apartment because you have children?

Briefly explain why you think your housing rights were denied and circle the factor(s) listed above that you believe apply.

3 Who do you believe discriminated against you?

For example: was it a landlord, owner, bank, real estate agent, broker, company, or organization?

Identify who you believe discriminated against you.

_____
Name

_____
Address

4 Where did the alleged act of discrimination occur?

For example: Was it at a rental unit? Single family home? Public or Assisted Housing? A Mobile Home?

Did it occur at a bank or other lending institution?

Provide the address.

_____
Address

_____
City   State   Zip Code

5 When did the last act of discrimination occur?

Enter the date

____/____/____

Is the alleged discrimination continuing or ongoing?   Yes No_____   _____

_____
Signature   Date

Send this form to HUD or to the fair housing agency nearest you. If you are unable to complete this form, you may call that office directly. See address and telephone listings on back page.

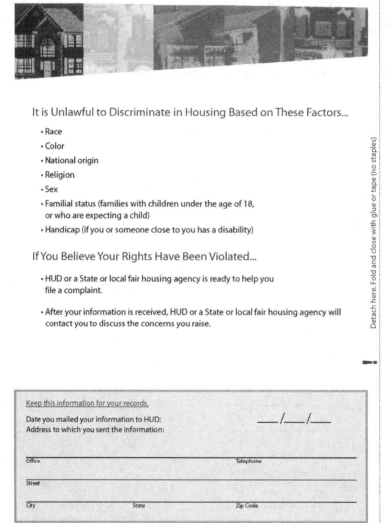

It is Unlawful to Discriminate in Housing Based on These Factors...

- Race
- Color
- National origin
- Religion
- Sex
- Familial status (families with children under the age of 18, or who are expecting a child)
- Handicap (if you or someone close to you has a disability)

If You Believe Your Rights Have Been Violated...

- HUD or a State or local fair housing agency is ready to help you file a complaint.

- After your information is received, HUD or a State or local fair housing agency will contact you to discuss the concerns you raise.

Detach here. Fold and close with glue or tape (no staples)

Keep this information for your records.

Date you mailed your information to HUD: ____ / ____ / ____
Address to which you sent the information:

Office _____ Telephone _____

Street _____

City _____ State _____ Zip Code _____

If you have not heard from HUD or a State or local fair housing agency within three weeks from the date you mailed this form, you may call to inquire about the status of your complaint. See address and telephone listings on back page.

ARE YOU A VICTIM OF HOUSING DISCRIMINATION?

"The American Dream of having a safe and decent place to call 'home' reflects our shared belief that in this nation,   opportunity and success are within everyone's reach.
Under our Fair Housing laws, every citizen is assured the opportunity to build a better life in the home or apartment of their choice — regardless of their race, color, religion, sex, national origin, family status or disability."

Alphonso Jackson
Secretary

HOW DO YOU RECOGNIZE HOUSING DISCRIMINATION?

Under the Fair Housing Act, it is Against the Law to:

- Refuse to rent to you or sell you housing
- Tell you housing is unavailable when in fact it is available
- Show you apartments or homes only in certain neighborhoods
- Set different terms, conditions, or privileges for sale or rental of a dwelling
- Provide different housing services or facilities
- Advertise housing to preferred groups of people only
- Refuse to provide you with information regarding mortgage loans, deny you a mortgage loan, or impose different terms or conditions on a mortgage loan
- Deny you property insurance
- Conduct property appraisals in a discriminatory manner
- Refuse to make reasonable accomodations for persons with a disability if the accommodation may be necessary to afford such person a reasonable and equal opportunity to use and enjoy a dwelling.
- Fail to design and construct housing in an accessible manner
- Harass, coerce, intimidate, or interfere with anyone exercising or assisting someone else with his/her fair housing rights

Fair Housing: Equal Opportunity for All

U.S. Department of Housing and Urban Development
Office of Fair Housing and Equal Opportunity

Fair Housing
Equal Opportunity for All

Please visit our website: www.hud.gov/fairhousing

Fair Housing - Equal Opportunity for All

America, in every way, represents equality of opportunity for all persons. The rich diversity of its citizens and the spirit of unity that binds us all symbolize the principles of freedom and justice upon which this nation was founded. That is why it is extremely disturbing when new immigrants, minorities, families with children, and persons with disabilities are denied the housing of their choice because of illegal discrimination.

The Department of Housing and Urban Development enforces the Fair Housing Act and the other federal laws that prohibit discrimination and the intimidation of people in their homes, apartment buildings, and condominium developments - and nearly all housing transactions, including the rental and sale of housing and the provision of mortgage loans.

Equal access to rental housing and homeownership opportunities is the cornerstone of this nation's federal housing policy. Landlords who refuse to rent or sell homes to people based on race, color, national origin, religion, sex, familial status, or disability are violating federal law, and HUD will vigorously pursue them.

Housing discrimination is not only illegal, it contradicts in every way the principles of freedom and opportunity we treasure as Americans. The Department of Housing and Urban Development is committed to ensuring that everyone is treated equally when searching for a place to call home.

Alphonso Jackson
Secretary

U.S. Department of Housing and Urban Development (HUD)
Secretary Alphonso Jackson
451 7th Street, S.W.
Washington, D.C. 20410-2000

The Fair Housing Act

The Fair Housing Act prohibits discrimination in housing because of:
- Race or color
- National origin
- Religion
- Gender
- Familial status (including children under the age of 18 living with parents or legal custodians; pregnant women and people securing custody of children under 18)
- Disability

What Housing Is Covered?

The Fair Housing Act covers most housing. In some circumstances, the Act exempts owner-occupied buildings with no more than four units, single-family housing sold or rented without the use of a broker and housing operated by organizations and private clubs that limit occupancy to members.

What Is Prohibited?

In the Sale and Rental of Housing: No one may take any of the following actions based on race, color, religion, gender, disability, familial status, or national origin:

- Refuse to rent or sell housing
- Refuse to negotiate for housing
- Make housing unavailable
- Deny a dwelling
- Set different terms, conditions or privileges for sale or rental of a dwelling
- Provide different housing services or facilities
- Falsely deny that housing is available for inspection, sale or rental
- For profit, persuade, or try to persuade homeowners to sell or rent dwellings by suggesting that people of a particular race, etc. have moved, or are about to move into the neighborhood (blockbusting) or
- Deny any person access to, or membership or participation in, any organization, facility or service (such as a multiple listing service) related to the sale or rental of dwellings, or discriminate against any person in the terms or conditions of such access, membership or participation.

In Mortgage Lending: No one may take any of the following actions based on race, color, religion, gender, disability, familial status, or national origin:

* Refuse to make a mortgage loan
* Refuse to provide information regarding loans
* Impose different terms or conditions on a loan, such as different interest rates, points, or fees
* Discriminate in appraising property
* Refuse to purchase a loan or
* Set different terms or conditions for purchasing a loan.

In Addition, it is a violation of the Fair Housing Act to:

* Threaten, coerce, intimidate or interfere with anyone exercising a fair housing right or assisting others who exercise that right
* Make, print, or publish any statement, in connection with the sale or rental of a dwelling, that indicates a preference, limitation, or discrimination based on race, color, religion, gender, disability, familial status, or national origin. This prohibition against discriminatory advertising applies to single-family and owner-occupied housing that is otherwise exempt from the Fair Housing Act.
* Refuse to provide homeowners insurance coverage for a dwelling because of the race, color, religion, gender, disability, familial status, or national origin of the owner and/or occupants of a dwelling
* Discriminate in the terms or conditions of homeowners insurance coverage because of the race, color, religion, gender, disability, familial status, or national origin of the owner and/or occupants of a dwelling
* Refuse to provide homeowners insurance, or imposing less favorable terms or conditions of coverage because of the predominant race, color, religion, gender, disability, familial status or national origin of the residents of the neighborhood in which a dwelling is located ("redlining")
* Refuse to provide available information on the full range of homeowners insurance coverage options available because of the race, etc. of the owner and/or occupants of a dwelling
* Make, print, or publish any statement, in connection with the provision of homeowners insurance coverage, that indicates a preference, limitation or discrimination based on race, color, religion, gender, disability, familial status or national origin.

Additional Protection If You Have a Disability

If you or someone associated with you:

- Have a physical or mental disability (including hearing, mobility and visual impairments, cancer, chronic mental illness, AIDS, AIDS Related Complex, or mental retardation) that substantially limits one or more major life activities
- Have a record of such a disability or
- Are regarded as having such a disability, your landlord may not:

  - Refuse to let you make reasonable modifications to your dwelling or common use areas, at your expense, if necessary for the disabled person to fully use the housing. (Where reasonable, the landlord may permit changes only if you agree to restore the property to its original condition when you move.)
  - Refuse to make reasonable accommodations in rules, policies, practices or services if necessary for the disabled person to use the housing on an equal basis with nondisabled persons.

Example: A building with a "no pets" policy must allow a visually impaired tenant to keep a guide dog.

Example: An apartment complex that offers tenants ample, unassigned parking must honor a request from a mobility-impaired tenant for a reserved space near her apartment if necessary to assure that she can have access to her apartment.

However, housing need not be made available to a person who is a direct threat to the health or safety of others or who currently uses illegal drugs.

Everything U Need to Know...

Accessibility Requirements for New Multifamily Buildings: In buildings with four or more units that were first occupied **after** March 13, 1991, and that have an elevator:

• Public and common areas must be accessible to persons with disabilities
• Doors and hallways must be wide enough for wheelchairs
• All units must have:
  - An accessible route into and through the unit
  - Accessible light switches, electrical outlets, thermostats and other environmental controls
  - Reinforced bathroom walls to allow later installation of grab bars and
  - Kitchens and bathrooms that can be used by people in wheelchairs.

If a building with four or more units has no elevator and was first occupied after March 13, 1991, these standards apply to ground floor units only.

These accessibility requirements for new multifamily buildings do not replace more stringent accessibility standards required under State or local law.

Housing Opportunities for Families with Children

The Fair Housing Act makes it unlawful to discriminate against a person whose household includes one or more children who are under 18 years of age ("*familial status*"). Familial status protection covers households in which one or more minor children live with:

- A parent;
- A person who has legal custody (including guardianship) of a minor child or children; or
- The designee of a parent or legal custodian, with the written permission of the parent or legal custodian.

Familial status protection also extends to pregnant women and any person in the process of securing legal custody of a minor child (including adoptive or foster parents).

Additional familial status protections:

You also may be covered under the familial status provisions of the Fair Housing Act if you experience retaliation, or suffer a financial loss (employment, housing, or realtor's commission) because:

- You sold or rented, or offered to sell or rent a dwelling to a family with minor children; or
- You negotiated, or attempted to negotiate the sale or rental of a dwelling to a family with minor children.

The "Housing for Older Persons" Exemption:

The Fair Housing Act specifically exempts some senior housing facilities and communities from liability for *familial status* discrimination. Exempt senior housing facilities or communities can <u>lawfully</u> refuse to sell or rent dwellings to families with minor children, or may impose different terms and conditions of residency. In order to qualify for the "housing for older persons" exemption, a facility or community must prove that its housing is:

- Provided under any State or Federal program that HUD has determined to be specifically designed and operated to assist *elderly persons* (as defined in the State or Federal program); or

5

- Intended for, and solely occupied by persons *62 years of age or older*; or
- Intended and operated for occupancy by persons *55 years of age or older.*

In order to qualify for the "**55 or older**" housing exemption, a facility or community must satisfy each of the following requirements:

- at least *80 percent* of the occupied units must have at least one occupant who is 55 years of age or older; and
- the facility or community must publish and adhere to policies and procedures that demonstrate the *intent* to operate as "55 or older" housing; and
- the facility or community must comply with HUD's regulatory requirements for *age verification* of residents by reliable surveys and affidavits.

The *"housing for older persons"* exemption does not protect senior housing facilities or communities from liability for housing discrimination based on *race, color, religion, gender, disability, or national origin.* Further, *"55 or older"* housing facilities or communities that do permit residency by families with minor children cannot lawfully *segregate* such families in a particular section, building, or portion of a building.

If You Think Your Rights Have Been Violated

HUD is ready to help with any problem of housing discrimination. If you think your rights have been violated, you may write a letter or telephone the HUD office nearest you. You have one year after the discrimination allegedly occurred or ended to file a complaint with HUD, but you should file it as soon as possible.

What to Tell HUD:

- Your name and address
- The name and address of the person your complaint is against (the respondent)
- The address or other identification of the housing involved
- A short description of the alleged violation (the event that caused you to believe your rights were violated)
- The date(s) of the alleged violation.

Where to Write or Call: Send a letter to the HUD office nearest you, or if you wish, you may call that office directly. The TTY numbers listed for those offices are not toll free. Or you may call the toll free national TTY hotline at 1-800-927-9275.

For Connecticut, Maine, Massachusetts, New Hampshire, Rhode Island and Vermont:

BOSTON REGIONAL OFFICE
(Complaints_office_01@hud.gov)
U.S. Department of Housing and Urban Development
Thomas P. O'Neill Jr. Federal Building
10 Causeway Street, Room 308
Boston, MA 02222-1092
Telephone (617) 994-8300 or 1-800-827-5005
Fax (617) 565-7313 * TTY (617) 565-5453

For New Jersey and New York:

NEW YORK REGIONAL OFFICE
(Complaints_office_02@hud.gov)
U.S. Department of Housing and Urban Development
26 Federal Plaza, Room 3532
New York, NY 10278-0068
Telephone (212) 542-7519 or 1-800-496-4294
Fax (212) 264-9829 * TTY (212) 264-0927

For Delaware, District of Columbia, Maryland, Pennsylvania, Virginia and West Virginia:

PHILADELPHIA REGIONAL OFFICE
(Complaints_office_03@hud.gov)
U.S. Department of Housing and Urban Development
The Wanamaker Building
100 Penn Square East
Philadelphia, PA 19107-9344
Telephone (215) 656-0663 or 1-888-799-2085
Fax (215) 656-3449 * TTY (215) 656-3450

For Alabama, Florida, Georgia, Kentucky,
Mississippi, North Carolina, Puerto Rico,
South Carolina, Tennessee
and the U.S. Virgin Islands:

ATLANTA REGIONAL OFFICE
(Complaints_office_04@hud.gov)
U.S. Department of Housing and Urban
Development
Five Points Plaza
40 Marietta Street, 16th Floor
Atlanta, GA 30303-2808
Telephone (404) 331-5140 or 1-800-440-8091
Fax (404) 331-1021 * TTY (404) 730-2654

For Illinois, Indiana, Michigan, Minnesota,
Ohio and Wisconsin:

CHICAGO REGIONAL OFFICE
(Complaints_office_05@hud.gov)
U.S. Department of Housing and Urban
Development
Ralph H. Metcalfe Federal Building
77 West Jackson Boulevard, Room 2101
Chicago, IL 60604-3507
Telephone (312) 353-7796 or 1-800-765-9372
Fax (312) 886-2837 * TTY (312) 353-7143

For Arkansas, Louisiana, New Mexico,
Oklahoma and Texas:

FORT WORTH REGIONAL OFFICE
(Complaints_office_06@hud.gov)
U.S. Department of Housing and Urban
Development
801 North Cherry, 27th Floor
Fort Worth, TX 76102-6803
Telephone (817) 978-5900 or 1-888-560-8913
Fax (817) 978-5876/5851 * TTY (817) 978-5595
Mailing Address:
U.S. Department of Housing and Urban
Development
Post Office Box 2905
Fort Worth, TX 76113-2905

8

For Iowa, Kansas, Missouri and Nebraska:

KANSAS CITY REGIONAL OFFICE
(Complaints_office_07@hud.gov)
U.S. Department of Housing and Urban
Development
Gateway Tower II,
400 State Avenue, Room 200, 4th Floor
Kansas City, KS 66101-2406
Telephone (913) 551-6958 or 1-800-743-5323
Fax (913) 551-6856 * TTY (913) 551-6972

For Colorado, Montana, North Dakota,
South Dakota, Utah and Wyoming:

DENVER REGIONAL OFFICE
(Complaints_office_08@hud.gov)
U.S. Department of Housing and Urban
Development
1670 Broadway
Denver, CO 80202-4801
Telephone (303) 672-5437 or 1-800-877-7353
Fax (303) 672-5026 * TTY (303) 672-5248

For Arizona, California, Hawaii and Nevada:

SAN FRANCISCO REGIONAL OFFICE
(Complaints_office_09@hud.gov)
U.S. Department of Housing and Urban
Development
600 Harrison Street, Third Floor
San Francisco, CA 94107-1387
Telephone (415) 489-6548 or 1-800-347-3739
Fax (415) 489-6558 * TTY (415) 489-6564

For Alaska, Idaho, Oregon and Washington:

SEATTLE REGIONAL OFFICE
(Complaints_office_10@hud.gov)
U.S. Department of Housing and Urban
Development
Seattle Federal Office Building
909 First Avenue, Room 205
Seattle, WA 98104-1000
Telephone (206) 220-5170 or 1-800-877-0246
Fax (206) 220-5447 * TTY (206) 220-5185

If after contacting the local office nearest you, you still have questions - you may contact HUD further at:

U.S. Department of Housing and Urban Development
Office of Fair Housing and Equal Opportunity
451 7th Street, S.W, Room 5204
Washington, DC 20410-2000
Telephone 1-800-669-9777
Fax (202) 708-1425 * TTY 1-800-927-9275

If You Are Disabled: HUD also provides:
• A TTY phone for the deaf/hard of hearing users (see above list for the nearest HUD office)
• Interpreters
• Tapes and braille materials
• Assistance in reading and completing forms

What Happens When You File A Complaint?

HUD will notify you in writing when your complaint is accepted for filing under the Fair Housing Act. HUD also will:

• Notify the alleged violator ("respondent") of the filing of your complaint, and allow the respondent time to submit a written answer to the complaint.
• Investigate your complaint, and determine whether or not there is reasonable cause to believe that the respondent violated the Fair Housing Act.
• Notify you and the respondent if HUD cannot complete its investigation within 100 days of filing your complaint, and provide reasons for the delay.

Fair Housing Act Conciliation: During the complaint investigation, HUD is required to offer you and the respondent the opportunity to voluntarily resolve your complaint with a HUD Conciliation Agreement. A HUD Conciliation Agreement provides individual relief for you, and protects the public interest by deterring future discrimination by the respondent. Once you and the respondent sign a HUD Conciliation Agreement, and HUD approves the Agreement, HUD will cease investigating your complaint. If you believe that the respondent has violated ("breached") your Conciliation Agreement, you should promptly notify the HUD Office that investigated your complaint. If HUD determines that there is reasonable cause to believe that the

respondent violated the Agreement, HUD will ask the U.S. Department of Justice to file suit against the respondent in Federal District Court to enforce the terms of the Agreement.

Complaint Referrals to State or Local Public Fair Housing Agencies: If HUD has certified that your State or local public fair housing agency enforces a civil rights law or ordinance that provides rights, remedies and protections that are *"substantially equivalent"* to the Fair Housing Act, HUD must promptly refer your complaint to that agency for investigation, and must promptly notify you of the referral. The State or local agency will investigate your complaint under the *"substantially equivalent"* State or local civil rights law or ordinance. The State or local public fair housing agency must start investigating your complaint within 30 days of HUD's referral, or HUD may retrieve ("reactivate") the complaint for investigation under the Fair Housing Act.

Does the U.S. Department of Justice Play a Role?

If you need immediate help to stop or prevent a severe problem caused by a Fair Housing Act violation, HUD may be able to assist you as soon as you file a complaint. HUD may authorize the U.S. Department of Justice to file a Motion in Federal District Court for a 10-day Temporary Restraining Order (TRO) against the respondent, followed by a Preliminary Injunction pending the outcome of HUD's investigation. A Federal Judge may grant a TRO or a Preliminary Injunction against a respondent in cases where:

- Irreparable (irreversible) harm or injury to housing rights is likely to occur without HUD's intervention, and
- There is substantial evidence that the respondent has violated the Fair Housing Act.

Example: An owner agrees to sell a house, but, after discovering that the buyers are black, pulls the house off the market, then promptly lists it for sale again. The buyers file a discrimination complaint with HUD. HUD may authorize the U.S. Department of Justice to seek an injunction in Federal District Court to prevent the owner from selling the house to anyone else until HUD investigates the complaint.

What Happens After A Complaint Investigation?

Determination of Reasonable Cause, Charge of Discrimination, and Election: When your complaint investigation is complete, HUD will prepare a Final Investigative Report summarizing the evidence gathered during the investigation. If HUD determines that there is reasonable cause to believe that the respondent(s) discriminated against you, HUD will issue a Determination of Reasonable Cause and a Charge of Discrimination against the respondent(s). You and the respondent(s) have Twenty (20) days after receiving notice of the Charge to decide ("elect") whether to have your case heard by a HUD Administrative Law Judge (ALJ) or to have a civil trial in Federal District Court.

HUD Administrative Law Judge Hearing: If neither you nor the respondent elects to have a Federal civil trial before the 20-day Election Period expires, HUD will promptly schedule a Hearing for your case before a HUD Administrative Law Judge. The ALJ Hearing will be conducted in the locality where the discrimination allegedly occurred. During the ALJ Hearing, you and the respondent(s) have the right to appear in person, to be represented by legal counsel, to present evidence, to cross-examine witnesses, and to request subpoenas in aid of discovery of evidence. HUD attorneys will represent you during the ALJ Hearing at no cost to you; however, you may also choose to intervene in the case and retain your own attorney. At the conclusion of the Hearing, the HUD ALJ will issue a Decision based on findings of fact and conclusions of law. If the HUD ALJ concludes that the respondent(s) violated the Fair Housing Act, the respondent(s) can be ordered to:

• Compensate you for actual damages.
• Provide permanent injunctive relief.
• Provide appropriate equitable relief (for example, make the housing available to you).
• Pay your reasonable attorney's fees.
• Pay a civil penalty to HUD to vindicate the public interest by discouraging future discriminatory housing practices. The maximum civil penalties are: **$11,000.00** for a first violation of the Act; **$32,500.00** if a previous violation has occurred within the preceding five-year period; and **$60,000.00** if two or more previous violations have occurred within the preceding seven-year period.

Civil Trial in Federal District Court: If either you or the respondent elects to have a Federal civil trial for your complaint, HUD must refer your case to the U.S. Department of Justice for enforcement. The U.S. Department of Justice will file a civil lawsuit on your behalf in the U.S. District Court in the circuit in which the discrimination allegedly occurred. You also may choose to intervene in the case and retain your own attorney. Either you or the respondent may request a jury trial, and you each have the right to appear in person, to be represented by legal counsel, to present evidence, to cross-examine witnesses, and to request subpoenas in aid of discovery of evidence. If the Federal Court decides in your favor, a Judge or jury may order the respondent(s) to:

- Compensate you for actual damages.
- Provide permanent injunctive relief.
- Provide appropriate equitable relief (for example, make the housing available to you).
- Pay your reasonable attorney's fees.
- Pay punitive damages to you.
- Pay a civil penalty to the U.S. Treasury to vindicate the public interest, in an amount not exceeding **$55,000.00** for a first violation of the Act and in an amount not exceeding **$110,000.00** for any subsequent violation of the Act.

Determination of No Reasonable Cause and Dismissal: If HUD finds that there is no reasonable cause to believe that the respondent(s) violated the Act, HUD will dismiss your complaint with a Determination of No Reasonable Cause. HUD will notify you and the respondent(s) of the dismissal by mail, and you may request a copy of the Final Investigative Report.

Reconsiderations of No Reasonable Cause Determinations: The Fair Housing Act provides no formal appeal process for complaints dismissed by HUD. However, if your complaint is dismissed with a Determination of No Reasonable Cause, you may submit a written request for a reconsideration review to: Director, FHEO Office of Enforcement, U.S .Department of Housing and Urban Development, 451-7th Street, SW, Room 5206, Washington, DC 20410-2000.

Department of Housing
and Urban Development
Room 5204
Washington, DC 20410-2000

You May File a Private Lawsuit: Even if HUD dismisses your complaint, the Fair Housing Act gives you the right to file a private civil lawsuit against the respondent(s) in Federal District Court. You must file your lawsuit within two (2) years of the most recent date of alleged discrimination. The time during which HUD was processing your complaint is not counted in the 2-year filing period. You must file your lawsuit at your own expense; however, if you cannot afford an attorney, the Court may appoint one for you.

Even if HUD is still processing your complaint, you may file a private civil lawsuit against the respondent, unless: (1) you have already signed a HUD Conciliation Agreement to resolve your HUD complaint; or (2) a HUD Administrative Law Judge has commenced an Administrative Hearing for your complaint.

Other Tools to Combat Housing Discrimination:

- If there is noncompliance with the order of an Administrative Law Judge, HUD may seek temporary relief, enforcement of the order or a restraining order in a United States Court of Appeals.
- The Attorney General may file a suit in Federal District Court if there is reasonable cause to believe a pattern or practice of housing discrimination is occurring.

For Further Information:

The purpose of this brochure is to summarize your right to fair housing. The Fair Housing Act and HUD's regulations contain more detail and technical information. If you need a copy of the law or regulations, contact the HUD Fair Housing Office nearest you. See the list of HUD Fair Housing Offices on pages 7-9.

HUD-1686-1-FHEO
February 2006
Previous Editions Obsolete

Lead-Based Paint Pamphlet

Are You Planning To Buy, Rent, or Renovate a Home Built Before 1978?

Many houses and apartments built before 1978 have paint that contains high levels of lead (called lead-based paint). Lead from paint, chips, and dust can pose serious health hazards if not taken care of properly.

OWNERS, BUYERS, and RENTERS are encouraged to check for lead (see page 6) before renting, buying or renovating pre-1978 housing.

Federal law requires that individuals receive certain information before renting, buying, or renovating pre-1978 housing:

LANDLORDS have to disclose known information on lead-based paint and lead-based paint hazards before leases take effect. Leases must include a disclosure about lead-based paint.

SELLERS have to disclose known information on lead-based paint and lead-based paint hazards before selling a house. Sales contracts must include a disclosure about lead-based paint. Buyers have up to 10 days to check for lead.

RENOVATORS disturbing more than 2 square feet of painted surfaces have to give you this pamphlet before starting work.

IMPORTANT!

Lead From Paint, Dust, and Soil Can Be Dangerous If Not Managed Properly

FACT: Lead exposure can harm young children and babies even before they are born.

FACT: Even children who seem healthy can have high levels of lead in their bodies.

FACT: People can get lead in their bodies by breathing or swallowing lead dust, or by eating soil or paint chips containing lead.

FACT: People have many options for reducing lead hazards. In most cases, lead-based paint that is in good condition is not a hazard.

FACT: Removing lead-based paint improperly can increase the danger to your family.

If you think your home might have lead hazards, read this pamphlet to learn some simple steps to protect your family.

Lead Gets in the Body in Many Ways

Childhood lead poisoning remains a major environmental health problem in the U.S.

Even children who appear healthy can have dangerous levels of lead in their bodies.

People can get lead in their body if they:

◆ Breathe in lead dust (especially during renovations that disturb painted surfaces).

◆ Put their hands or other objects covered with lead dust in their mouths.

◆ Eat paint chips or soil that contains lead.

Lead is even more dangerous to children under the age of 6:

◆ At this age children's brains and nervous systems are more sensitive to the damaging effects of lead.

◆ Children's growing bodies absorb more lead.

◆ Babies and young children often put their hands and other objects in their mouths. These objects can have lead dust on them.

Lead is also dangerous to women of childbearing age:

◆ Women with a high lead level in their system prior to pregnancy would expose a fetus to lead through the placenta during fetal development.

2

Lead's Effects

It is important to know that even exposure to low levels of lead can severely harm children.

In children, lead can cause:

◆ Nervous system and kidney damage.

◆ Learning disabilities, attention deficit disorder, and decreased intelligence.

◆ Speech, language, and behavior problems.

◆ Poor muscle coordination.

◆ Decreased muscle and bone growth.

◆ Hearing damage.

While low-lead exposure is most common, exposure to high levels of lead can have devastating effects on children, including seizures, unconsciousness, and, in some cases, death.

Although children are especially susceptible to lead exposure, lead can be dangerous for adults too.

In adults, lead can cause:

◆ Increased chance of illness during pregnancy.

◆ Harm to a fetus, including brain damage or death.

◆ Fertility problems (in men and women).

◆ High blood pressure.

◆ Digestive problems.

◆ Nerve disorders.

◆ Memory and concentration problems.

◆ Muscle and joint pain.

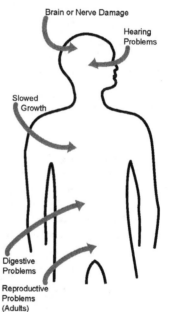

Brain or Nerve Damage

Hearing Problems

Slowed Growth

Digestive Problems

Reproductive Problems (Adults)

Lead affects the body in many ways.

3

Where Lead-Based Paint Is Found

In general, the older your home, the more likely it has lead-based paint.

Many homes built before 1978 have lead-based paint. The federal government banned lead-based paint from housing in 1978. Some states stopped its use even earlier. Lead can be found:

◆ In homes in the city, country, or suburbs.

◆ In apartments, single-family homes, and both private and public housing.

◆ Inside and outside of the house.

◆ In soil around a home. (Soil can pick up lead from exterior paint or other sources such as past use of leaded gas in cars.)

Checking Your Family for Lead

Get your children and home tested if you think your home has high levels of lead.

To reduce your child's exposure to lead, get your child checked, have your home tested (especially if your home has paint in poor condition and was built before 1978), and fix any hazards you may have. Children's blood lead levels tend to increase rapidly from 6 to 12 months of age, and tend to peak at 18 to 24 months of age.

Consult your doctor for advice on testing your children. A simple blood test can detect high levels of lead. Blood tests are usually recommended for:

◆ Children at ages 1 and 2.

◆ Children or other family members who have been exposed to high levels of lead.

◆ Children who should be tested under your state or local health screening plan.

Your doctor can explain what the test results mean and if more testing will be needed.

4

Identifying Lead Hazards

Lead-based paint is usually not a hazard if it is in good condition, and it is not on an impact or friction surface, like a window. It is defined by the federal government as paint with lead levels greater than or equal to 1.0 milligram per square centimeter, or more than 0.5% by weight.

Deteriorating lead-based paint (peeling, chipping, chalking, cracking or damaged) is a hazard and needs immediate attention. It may also be a hazard when found on surfaces that children can chew or that get a lot of wear-and-tear, such as:

◆ Windows and window sills.

◆ Doors and door frames.

◆ Stairs, railings, banisters, and porches.

Lead from paint chips, which you can see, and lead dust, which you can't always see, can both be serious hazards.

Lead dust can form when lead-based paint is scraped, sanded, or heated. Dust also forms when painted surfaces bump or rub together. Lead chips and dust can get on surfaces and objects that people touch. Settled lead dust can re-enter the air when people vacuum, sweep, or walk through it. The following two federal standards have been set for lead hazards in dust:

◆ 40 micrograms per square foot ($\mu g/ft^2$) and higher for floors, including carpeted floors.

◆ 250 $\mu g/ft^2$ and higher for interior window sills.

Lead in soil can be a hazard when children play in bare soil or when people bring soil into the house on their shoes. The following two federal standards have been set for lead hazards in residential soil:

◆ 400 parts per million (ppm) and higher in play areas of bare soil.

◆ 1,200 ppm (average) and higher in bare soil in the remainder of the yard.

The only way to find out if paint, dust and soil lead hazards exist is to test for them. The next page describes the most common methods used.

5

Everything U Need to Know...™

Checking Your Home for Lead

Just knowing that a home has lead-based paint may not tell you if there is a hazard.

You can get your home tested for lead in several different ways:

◆ A paint **inspection** tells you whether your home has lead-based paint and where it is located. It won't tell you whether or not your home currently has lead hazards.

◆ A **risk assessment** tells you if your home currently has any lead hazards from lead in paint, dust, or soil. It also tells you what actions to take to address any hazards.

◆ A combination risk assessment and inspection tells you if your home has any lead hazards and if your home has any lead-based paint, and where the lead-based paint is located.

Hire a trained and certified testing professional who will use a range of reliable methods when testing your home.

◆ Visual inspection of paint condition and location.

◆ A portable x-ray fluorescence (XRF) machine.

◆ Lab tests of paint, dust, and soil samples.

There are state and federal programs in place to ensure that testing is done safely, reliably, and effectively. Contact your state or local agency (see bottom of page 11) for more information, or call **1-800-424-LEAD (5323)** for a list of contacts in your area.

Home test kits for lead are available, but may not always be accurate. Consumers should not rely on these kits before doing renovations or to assure safety.

What You Can Do Now To Protect Your Family

If you suspect that your house has lead hazards, you can take some immediate steps to reduce your family's risk:

◆ **If you rent, notify your landlord of peeling or chipping paint.**

◆ **Clean up paint chips immediately.**

◆ **Clean floors, window frames, window sills, and other surfaces weekly.** Use a mop or sponge with warm water and a general all-purpose cleaner or a cleaner made specifically for lead. REMEMBER: NEVER MIX AMMONIA AND BLEACH PRODUCTS TOGETHER SINCE THEY CAN FORM A DANGEROUS GAS.

◆ **Thoroughly rinse sponges and mop heads after cleaning dirty or dusty areas.**

◆ **Wash children's hands often, especially before they eat and before nap time and bed time.**

◆ **Keep play areas clean.** Wash bottles, pacifiers, toys, and stuffed animals regularly.

◆ **Keep children from chewing window sills or other painted surfaces.**

◆ **Clean or remove shoes before entering your home to avoid tracking in lead from soil.**

◆ **Make sure children eat nutritious, low-fat meals high in iron and calcium,** such as spinach and dairy products. Children with good diets absorb less lead.

7

Reducing Lead Hazards In The Home

Removing lead improperly can increase the hazard to your family by spreading even more lead dust around the house.

Always use a professional who is trained to remove lead hazards safely.

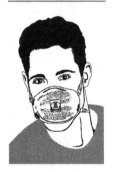

In addition to day-to-day cleaning and good nutrition:

◆ You can **temporarily** reduce lead hazards by taking actions such as repairing damaged painted surfaces and planting grass to cover soil with high lead levels. These actions (called "interim controls") are not permanent solutions and will need ongoing attention.

◆ To **permanently** remove lead hazards, you should hire a certified lead "abatement" contractor. Abatement (or permanent hazard elimination) methods include removing, sealing, or enclosing lead-based paint with special materials. Just painting over the hazard with regular paint is not permanent removal.

Always hire a person with special training for correcting lead problems—someone who knows how to do this work safely and has the proper equipment to clean up thoroughly. Certified contractors will employ qualified workers and follow strict safety rules as set by their state or by the federal government.

Once the work is completed, dust cleanup activities must be repeated until testing indicates that lead dust levels are below the following:

◆ 40 micrograms per square foot ($\mu g/ft^2$) for floors, including carpeted floors;

◆ 250 $\mu g/ft^2$ for interior windows sills; and

◆ 400 $\mu g/ft^2$ for window troughs.

Call your state or local agency (see bottom of page 11) for help in locating certified professionals in your area and to see if financial assistance is available.

Remodeling or Renovating a Home With Lead-Based Paint

Take precautions before your contractor or you begin remodeling or renovating anything that disturbs painted surfaces (such as scraping off paint or tearing out walls):

◆ **Have the area tested for lead-based paint.**

◆ **Do not use a belt-sander, propane torch, high temperature heat gun, dry scraper, or dry sandpaper** to remove lead-based paint. These actions create large amounts of lead dust and fumes. Lead dust can remain in your home long after the work is done.

◆ **Temporarily move your family** (especially children and pregnant women) out of the apartment or house until the work is done and the area is properly cleaned. If you can't move your family, at least completely seal off the work area.

◆ **Follow other safety measures to reduce lead hazards.** You can find out about other safety measures by calling 1-800-424-LEAD. Ask for the brochure "Reducing Lead Hazards When Remodeling Your Home." This brochure explains what to do before, during, and after renovations.

If you have already completed renovations or remodeling that could have released lead-based paint or dust, get your young children tested and follow the steps outlined on page 7 of this brochure.

If not conducted properly, certain types of renovations can release lead from paint and dust into the air.

9

Other Sources of Lead

While paint, dust, and soil are the most common sources of lead, other lead sources also exist.

◆ **Drinking water.** Your home might have plumbing with lead or lead solder. Call your local health department or water supplier to find out about testing your water. You cannot see, smell, or taste lead, and boiling your water will not get rid of lead. If you think your plumbing might have lead in it:

- Use only cold water for drinking and cooking.

- Run water for 15 to 30 seconds before drinking it, especially if you have not used your water for a few hours.

◆ **The job.** If you work with lead, you could bring it home on your hands or clothes. Shower and change clothes before coming home. Launder your work clothes separately from the rest of your family's clothes.

◆ Old painted **toys** and **furniture.**

◆ Food and liquids stored in **lead crystal** or **lead-glazed pottery or porcelain.**

◆ **Lead smelters** or other industries that release lead into the air.

◆ **Hobbies** that use lead, such as making pottery or stained glass, or refinishing furniture.

◆ **Folk remedies** that contain lead, such as "greta" and "azarcon" used to treat an upset stomach.

10

For More Information

The National Lead Information Center

Call **1-800-424-LEAD (424-5323)** to learn how to protect children from lead poisoning and for other information on lead hazards. To access lead information via the web, visit **www.epa.gov/lead** and **www.hud.gov/offices/lead/.**

EPA's Safe Drinking Water Hotline

Call **1-800-426-4791** for information about lead in drinking water.

Consumer Product Safety Commission (CPSC) Hotline

To request information on lead in consumer products, or to report an unsafe consumer product or a product-related injury call **1-800-638-2772**, or visit CPSC's Web site at: **www.cpsc.gov.**

Health and Environmental Agencies

Some cities, states, and tribes have their own rules for lead-based paint activities. Check with your local agency to see which laws apply to you. Most agencies can also provide information on finding a lead abatement firm in your area, and on possible sources of financial aid for reducing lead hazards. Receive up-to-date address and phone information for your local contacts on the Internet at **www.epa.gov/lead** or contact the National Lead Information Center at **1-800-424-LEAD.**

> For the hearing impaired, call the Federal Information Relay Service at **1-800-877-8339** to access any of the phone numbers in this brochure.

EPA Regional Offices

Your Regional EPA Office can provide further information regarding regulations and lead protection programs.

EPA Regional Offices

Region 1 (Connecticut, Massachusetts, Maine, New Hampshire, Rhode Island, Vermont)

Regional Lead Contact
U.S. EPA Region 1
Suite 1100 (CPT)
One Congress Street
Boston, MA 02114-2023
1 (888) 372-7341

Region 2 (New Jersey, New York, Puerto Rico, Virgin Islands)

Regional Lead Contact
U.S. EPA Region 2
2890 Woodbridge Avenue
Building 209, Mail Stop 225
Edison, NJ 08837-3679
(732) 321-6671

Region 3 (Delaware, Maryland, Pennsylvania, Virginia, Washington DC, West Virginia)

Regional Lead Contact
U.S. EPA Region 3 (3WC33)
1650 Arch Street
Philadelphia, PA 19103
(215) 814-5000

Region 4 (Alabama, Florida, Georgia, Kentucky, Mississippi, North Carolina, South Carolina, Tennessee)

Regional Lead Contact
U.S. EPA Region 4
61 Forsyth Street, SW
Atlanta, GA 30303
(404) 562-8998

Region 5 (Illinois, Indiana, Michigan, Minnesota, Ohio, Wisconsin)

Regional Lead Contact
U.S. EPA Region 5 (DT-8J)
77 West Jackson Boulevard
Chicago, IL 60604-3666
(312) 886-6003

Region 6 (Arkansas, Louisiana, New Mexico, Oklahoma, Texas)

Regional Lead Contact
U.S. EPA Region 6
1445 Ross Avenue, 12th Floor
Dallas, TX 75202-2733
(214) 665-7577

Region 7 (Iowa, Kansas, Missouri, Nebraska)

Regional Lead Contact
U.S. EPA Region 7
(ARTD-RALI)
901 N. 5th Street
Kansas City, KS 66101
(913) 551-7020

Region 8 (Colorado, Montana, North Dakota, South Dakota, Utah, Wyoming)

Regional Lead Contact
U.S. EPA Region 8
999 18th Street, Suite 500
Denver, CO 80202-2466
(303) 312-6021

Region 9 (Arizona, California, Hawaii, Nevada)

Regional Lead Contact
U.S. Region 9
75 Hawthorne Street
San Francisco, CA 94105
(415) 947-4164

Region 10 (Alaska, Idaho, Oregon, Washington)

Regional Lead Contact
U.S. EPA Region 10
Toxics Section WCM-128
1200 Sixth Avenue
Seattle, WA 98101-1128
(206) 553-1985

CPSC Regional Offices

Your Regional CPSC Office can provide further information regarding regulations and consumer product safety.

Eastern Regional Center
Consumer Product Safety Commission
201 Varick Street, Room 903
New York, NY 10014
(212) 620-4120

Western Regional Center
Consumer Product Safety Commission
1301 Clay Street, Suite 610-N
Oakland, CA 94612
(510) 637-4050

Central Regional Center
Consumer Product Safety Commission
230 South Dearborn Street, Room 2944
Chicago, IL 60604
(312) 353-8260

HUD Lead Office

Please contact HUD's Office of Healthy Homes and Lead Hazard Control for information on lead regulations, outreach efforts, and lead hazard control and research grant programs.

U.S. Department of Housing and Urban Development
Office of Healthy Homes and Lead Hazard Control
451 Seventh Street, SW, P-3206
Washington, DC 20410
(202) 755-1785

U.S. EPA Washington DC 20460   EPA747-K-99-001
U.S. CPSC Washington DC 20207   June 2003
U.S. HUD Washington DC 20410

Lead-Based Paint Disclosure

Disclosure of Information on Lead-Based Paint and/or Lead-Based Paint Hazards

Lead Warning Statement

Housing built before 1978 may contain lead-based paint. Lead from paint, paint chips, and dust can pose health hazards if not managed properly. Lead exposure is especially harmful to young children and pregnant women. Before renting pre-1978 housing, lessors must disclose the presence of known lead-based paint and/or lead-based paint hazards in the dwelling. Lessees must also receive a federally approved pamphlet on lead poisoning prevention.

Lessor's Disclosure

(a) Presence of lead-based paint and/or lead-based paint hazards (check (i) or (ii) below):

　　(i) _____ Known lead-based paint and/or lead-based paint hazards are present in the housing (explain).

　　_____

　　_____

　　(ii) _____ Lessor has no knowledge of lead-based paint and/or lead-based paint hazards in the housing.

(b) Records and reports available to the lessor (check (i) or (ii) below):

　　(i) _____ Lessor has provided the lessee with all available records and reports pertaining to lead-based paint and/or lead-based paint hazards in the housing (list documents below).

　　_____

　　_____

　　(ii) _____ Lessor has no reports or records pertaining to lead-based paint and/or lead-based paint hazards in the housing.

Lessee's Acknowledgment (initial)

(c) _____ Lessee has received copies of all information listed above.

(d) _____ Lessee has received the pamphlet *Protect Your Family from Lead in Your Home.*

Agent's Acknowledgment (initial)

(e) _____ Agent has informed the lessor of the lessor's obligations under 42 U.S.C. 4852d and is aware of his/her responsibility to ensure compliance.

Certification of Accuracy

The following parties have reviewed the information above and certify, to the best of their knowledge, that the information they have provided is true and accurate.

Lessor	Date	Lessor	Date
Lessee	Date	Lessee	Date
Agent	Date	Agent	Date

FCRA Summary of Rights

AmerUSA Corporation
3665 East Bay Drive #204-183
Largo, Florida 33771
Ph 727.467.0908 Fx 727.467.0918

FCRA

FCRA Summary of Rights

A Summary of Your Rights - Under the Fair Credit Reporting Act

The federal Fair Credit Reporting Act (FCRA) is designed to promote accuracy, fairness, and privacy of information in the files of every "consumer reporting agency" (CRA). Most CRAs are credit bureaus that gather and sell information about you -- such as if you pay your bills on time or have filed bankruptcy -- to creditors, employers, landlords, and other businesses. You can find the complete text of the FCRA, 15 U.S.C. §§1681-1681u, by visiting www.ftc.gov. The FCRA gives you specific rights, as outlined below. You may have additional rights under state law. You may contact a state or local consumer protection agency or a state attorney general to learn those rights.

- **You must be told if information in your file has been used against you.** Anyone who uses information from a CRA to take action against you -- such as denying an application for credit, insurance, or employment -- must tell you, and give you the name, address, and phone number of the CRA that provided the consumer report.

- **You can find out what is in your file.** At your request, a CRA must give you the information in your file, and a list of everyone who has requested it recently. There is no charge for the report if a person has taken action against you because of information supplied by the CRA, if you request the report within 60 days of receiving notice of the action. You also are entitled to one free report every twelve months upon request if you certify that (1) you are unemployed and plan to seek employment within 60 days, (2) you are on welfare, or (3) your report is inaccurate due to fraud. Otherwise, a CRA may charge you up to eight dollars.

- **You can dispute inaccurate information with the CRA.** If you tell a CRA that your file contains inaccurate information, the CRA must investigate the items (usually within 30 days) by presenting to its information source all relevant evidence you submit, unless your dispute is frivolous. The source must review your evidence and report its findings to the CRA. (The source also must advise national CRAs -- to which it has provided the data -- of any error.) The CRA must give you a written report of the investigation, and a copy of your report if the investigation results in any change. If the CRA's investigation does not resolve the dispute, you may add a brief statement to your file. The CRA must normally include a summary of your statement in future reports. If an item is deleted or a dispute statement is filed, you may ask that anyone who has recently received your report be notified of the change.

- **Inaccurate information must be corrected or deleted.** A CRA must remove or correct inaccurate or unverified information from its files, usually within 30 days after you dispute it. However, the CRA is not required to remove accurate data from your file unless it is outdated (as described below) or cannot be verified. If your dispute results in any change to your report, the CRA cannot reinsert into your file a disputed item unless the information source verifies its accuracy and completeness. In addition, the CRA must give you a written notice telling you it has reinserted the item. The notice must include the name, address and phone number of the information source.

- **You can dispute inaccurate items with the source of the information.** If you tell anyone -- such as a creditor who reports to a CRA -- that you dispute an item, they may not then report the information to a CRA without including a notice of your dispute. In addition, once you've notified the source of the error in writing, it may not continue to report the information if it is, in fact, an error.

- **Outdated information may not be reported.** In most cases, a CRA may not report negative information that is more than seven years old; ten years for bankruptcies.

- **Access to your file is limited.** A CRA may provide information about you only to people with a need recognized by the FCRA -- usually to consider an application with a creditor, insurer, employer, landlord, or other business.

- **Your consent is required for reports that are provided to employers, or reports that contain medical information.** A CRA may not give out information about you to your employer, or prospective employer, without your written consent. A CRA may not report medical information about you to creditors, insurers, or employers without your permission.

- **You may choose to exclude your name from CRA lists for unsolicited credit and insurance offers.** Creditors and insurers may use file information as the basis for sending you unsolicited offers of credit or insurance. Such offers must include a toll-free phone number for you to call if you want your name and address removed from future lists. If you call, you must be kept off the lists for two years. If you request, complete, and return the CRA form provided for this purpose, you must be taken off the lists indefinitely.

- **You may seek damages from violators.** If a CRA, a user or (in some cases) a provider of CRA data, violates the FCRA, you may sue them in state or federal court.

FOR QUESTIONS OR CONCERNS PLEASE CONTACT

Federal Trade Commission
Consumer Response Center- FCRA
Washington, DC 20580 * 202-326-3761

FHA:
The Fair Housing Act

The Fair Housing Act

FAIR HOUSING ACT

Sec. 800. [42 U.S.C. 3601 note] Short Title

This title may be cited as the "Fair Housing Act".

Sec. 801. [42 U.S.C. 3601] Declaration of Policy

It is the policy of the United States to provide, within constitutional limitations, for fair housing throughout the United States.

Sec. 802. [42 U.S.C. 3602] Definitions

As used in this subchapter--

(a) "Secretary" means the Secretary of Housing and Urban Development.

(b) "Dwelling" means any building, structure, or portion thereof which is occupied as, or designed or intended for occupancy as, a residence by one or more families, and any vacant land which is offered for sale or lease for the construction or location thereon of any such building, structure, or portion thereof.

(c) "Family" includes a single individual.

(d) "Person" includes one or more individuals, corporations, partnerships, associations, labor organizations, legal representatives, mutual companies, joint-stock companies, trusts, unincorporated organizations, trustees, trustees in cases under title 11 [of the United States Code], receivers, and fiduciaries.

(e) "To rent" includes to lease, to sublease, to let and otherwise to grant for a consideration the right to occupy premises not owned by the occupant.

(f) "Discriminatory housing practice" means an act that is unlawful under section 804, 805, 806, or 818 of this title.

(g) "State" means any of the several States, the District of Columbia, the Commonwealth of Puerto Rico, or any of the territories and possessions of the United States.

(h) "Handicap" means, with respect to a person--

(1) a physical or mental impairment which substantially limits one or more of such person's major life activities,

(2) a record of having such an impairment, or

(3) being regarded as having such an impairment, but such term does not include current, illegal use of or addiction to a controlled substance (as defined in section 102 of the Controlled Substances Act (21 U.S.C. 802)).

(i) "Aggrieved person" includes any person who--

(1) claims to have been injured by a discriminatory housing practice; or

(2) believes that such person will be injured by a discriminatory housing practice that is about to occur.

(j) "Complainant" means the person (including the Secretary) who files a complaint under section 810.

(k) "Familial status" means one or more individuals (who have not attained the age of 18 years) being domiciled with--

(1) a parent or another person having legal custody of such individual or individuals; or

(2) the designee of such parent or other person having such custody, with the written permission of such parent or other person.

The protections afforded against discrimination on the basis of familial status shall apply to any person who is pregnant or is in the process of securing legal custody of any individual who has not attained the age of 18 years.

(l) "Conciliation" means the attempted resolution of issues raised by a complaint, or by the investigation of such complaint, through informal negotiations involving the aggrieved person, the respondent, and the Secretary.

(m) "Conciliation agreement" means a written agreement setting forth the resolution of the issues in conciliation.

(n) "Respondent" means--

(1) the person or other entity accused in a complaint of an unfair housing practice; and

(2) any other person or entity identified in the course of investigation and notified as required with respect to respondents so identified under section 810(a).

(o) "Prevailing party" has the same meaning as such term has in section 722 of the Revised Statutes of the United States (42 U.S.C. 1988).

[42 U.S.C. 3602 note] Neither the term "individual with handicaps" nor the term "handicap" shall apply to an individual solely because that individual is a transvestite.

Sec. 803. [42 U.S.C. 3603] Effective dates of certain prohibitions

(a) Subject to the provisions of subsection (b) of this section and section 807 of this title, the prohibitions against discrimination in the sale or rental of housing set forth in section 804 of this title shall apply:

(1) Upon enactment of this subchapter, to--

(A) dwellings owned or operated by the Federal Government;

(B) dwellings provided in whole or in part with the aid of loans, advances, grants, or contributions made by the Federal Government, under agreements entered into after November 20, 1962, unless payment due thereon has been made in full prior to April 11, 1968;

(C) dwellings provided in whole or in part by loans insured, guaranteed, or otherwise secured by the credit of the Federal Government, under agreements entered into after November 20, 1962, unless payment thereon has been made in full prior to April 11, 1968: **Provided**, That nothing contained in subparagraphs (B) and (C) of this subsection shall be applicable to dwellings solely by virtue of the fact that they are subject to mortgages held by an FDIC or FSLIC institution; and

(D) dwellings provided by the development or the redevelopment of real property purchased, rented, or otherwise obtained from a State or local public agency receiving Federal financial assistance for slum clearance or urban renewal with respect to such real property under loan or grant contracts entered into after November 20, 1962.

(2) After December 31, 1968, to all dwellings covered by paragraph (1) and to all other dwellings except as exempted by subsection (b) of this section.

(b)Nothing in section 804 of this title (other than subsection (c)) shall apply to--

(1) any single-family house sold or rented by an owner: **Provided**, That such private individual owner does not own more than three such single-family houses at any one time: **Provided further**, That in the case of the sale of any such single-family house by a private individual owner not residing in such house at the time of such sale or who was not the most recent resident of such house prior to such sale, the exemption granted by this subsection shall apply only with respect to one such sale within any twenty-four month period: **Provided further**, That such bona fide private individual owner does not own any interest in, nor is there owned or reserved on his behalf, under any express or voluntary agreement, title to or any right to all or a portion of the proceeds from the sale or rental of, more than three such single-family houses at any one time: **Provided further**, That after December 31, 1969, the sale or rental of any such single-family house shall be excepted from the application of this subchapter only if such house is sold or rented (A) without the use in any manner of the sales or rental facilities or the sales or rental services of any real estate broker, agent, or salesman, or of such facilities or services of any person in the business of selling or renting dwellings, or of any employee or agent of any such broker, agent, salesman, or person and (B) without the publication, posting or mailing, after notice, of any advertisement or written notice in violation of section 804(c) of this title; but nothing in this proviso shall prohibit the use of attorneys, escrow agents, abstractors, title companies, and other such professional assistance as necessary to perfect or transfer the title, or

(2)rooms or units in dwellings containing living quarters occupied or intended to be occupied by no more than four families living independently of each other, if the owner actually maintains and occupies one of such living quarters as his residence.

(c)For the purposes of subsection (b) of this section, a person shall be deemed to be in the business of selling or renting dwellings if--

(1) he has, within the preceding twelve months, participated as principal in three or more transactions involving the sale or rental of any dwelling or any interest therein, or

(2) he has, within the preceding twelve months, participated as agent, other than in the sale of his own personal residence in providing sales or rental facilities or sales or rental services in two or more transactions involving the sale or rental of any dwelling or any interest therein, or

(3) he is the owner of any dwelling designed or intended for occupancy by, or occupied by, five or more families.

Sec. 804. [42 U.S.C. 3604] Discrimination in sale or rental of housing and other prohibited practices

As made applicable by section 803 of this title and except as exempted by sections 803(b) and 807 of this title, it shall be unlawful--

(a) To refuse to sell or rent after the making of a bona fide offer, or to refuse to negotiate for the sale or rental of, or otherwise make unavailable or deny, a dwelling to any person because of race, color, religion, sex, familial status, or national origin.

(b) To discriminate against any person in the terms, conditions, or privileges of sale or rental of a dwelling, or in the provision of services or facilities in connection therewith, because of race, color, religion, sex, familial status, or national origin.

(c) To make, print, or publish, or cause to be made, printed, or published any notice, statement, or advertisement, with respect to the sale or rental of a dwelling that indicates any preference, limitation, or discrimination based on race, color, religion, sex, handicap, familial status, or national origin, or an intention to make any such preference, limitation, or discrimination.

(d) To represent to any person because of race, color, religion, sex, handicap, familial status, or national origin that any dwelling is not available for inspection, sale, or rental when such dwelling is in fact so available.

(e) For profit, to induce or attempt to induce any person to sell or rent any dwelling by representations regarding the entry or prospective entry into the neighborhood of a person or persons of a particular race, color, religion, sex, handicap, familial status, or national origin.

(f)

(1) To discriminate in the sale or rental, or to otherwise make unavailable or deny, a dwelling to any buyer or renter because of a handicap of--

(A) that buyer or renter,

(B) a person residing in or intending to reside in that dwelling after it is so sold, rented, or made available; or

(C) any person associated with that buyer or renter.

(2) To discriminate against any person in the terms, conditions, or privileges of sale or

rental of a dwelling, or in the provision of services or facilities in connection with such dwelling, because of a handicap of--

(A) that person; or

(B) a person residing in or intending to reside in that dwelling after it is so sold, rented, or made available; or

(C) any person associated with that person.

(3) For purposes of this subsection, discrimination includes--

(A) a refusal to permit, at the expense of the handicapped person, reasonable modifications of existing premises occupied or to be occupied by such person if such modifications may be necessary to afford such person full enjoyment of the premises, except that, in the case of a rental, the landlord may where it is reasonable to do so condition permission for a modification on the renter agreeing to restore the interior of the premises to the condition that existed before the modification, reasonable wear and tear excepted.

(B) a refusal to make reasonable accommodations in rules, policies, practices, or services, when such accommodations may be necessary to afford such person equal opportunity to use and enjoy a dwelling; or

(C) in connection with the design and construction of covered multifamily dwellings for first occupancy after the date that is 30 months after the date of enactment of the Fair Housing Amendments Act of 1988, a failure to design and construct those dwelling in such a manner that--

(i) the public use and common use portions of such dwellings are readily accessible to and usable by handicapped persons;

(ii) all the doors designed to allow passage into and within all premises within such dwellings are sufficiently wide to allow passage by handicapped persons in wheelchairs; and

(iii) all premises within such dwellings contain the following features of adaptive design:

(I) an accessible route into and through the dwelling;

(II) light switches, electrical outlets, thermostats, and other environmental controls in accessible locations;

(III) reinforcements in bathroom walls to allow later installation of grab bars; and

(IV) usable kitchens and bathrooms such that an individual in a wheelchair can maneuver about the space.

(4) Compliance with the appropriate requirements of the American National Standard for buildings and facilities providing accessibility and usability for physically handicapped people (commonly cited as "ANSI A117.1") suffices to satisfy the requirements of paragraph (3)(C)(iii).

(5)

    (A) If a State or unit of general local government has incorporated into its laws the requirements set forth in paragraph (3)(C), compliance with such laws shall be deemed to satisfy the requirements of that paragraph.

    (B) A State or unit of general local government may review and approve newly constructed covered multifamily dwellings for the purpose of making determinations as to whether the design and construction requirements of paragraph (3)(C) are met.

    (C) The Secretary shall encourage, but may not require, States and units of local government to include in their existing procedures for the review and approval of newly constructed covered multifamily dwellings, determinations as to whether the design and construction of such dwellings are consistent with paragraph (3)(C), and shall provide technical assistance to States and units of local government and other persons to implement the requirements of paragraph (3)(C).

    (D) Nothing in this title shall be construed to require the Secretary to review or approve the plans, designs or construction of all covered multifamily dwellings, to determine whether the design and construction of such dwellings are consistent with the requirements of paragraph 3(C).

(6)

    (A) Nothing in paragraph (5) shall be construed to affect the authority and responsibility of the Secretary or a State or local public agency certified pursuant to section 810(f)(3) of this Act to receive and process complaints or otherwise engage in enforcement activities under this title.

    (B) Determinations by a State or a unit of general local government under paragraphs (5)(A) and (B) shall not be conclusive in enforcement proceedings under this title.

(7) As used in this subsection, the term "covered multifamily dwellings" means--

    (A) buildings consisting of 4 or more units if such buildings have one or more elevators; and

    (B) ground floor units in other buildings consisting of 4 or more units.

(8) Nothing in this title shall be construed to invalidate or limit any law of a State or political subdivision of a State, or other jurisdiction in which this title shall be effective, that requires dwellings to be designed and constructed in a manner that affords handicapped persons greater access than is required by this title.

(9) Nothing in this subsection requires that a dwelling be made available to an individual

whose tenancy would constitute a direct threat to the health or safety of other individuals or whose tenancy would result in substantial physical damage to the property of others.

Sec. 805. [42 U.S.C. 3605] Discrimination in Residential Real Estate-Related Transactions

(a) In General.--It shall be unlawful for any person or other entity whose business includes engaging in residential real estate-related transactions to discriminate against any person in making available such a transaction, or in the terms or conditions of such a transaction, because of race, color, religion, sex, handicap, familial status, or national origin.

(b) Definition.--As used in this section, the term "residential real estate-related transaction" means any of the following:

(1) The making or purchasing of loans or providing other financial assistance--

(A) for purchasing, constructing, improving, repairing, or maintaining a dwelling; or

(B) secured by residential real estate.

(2) The selling, brokering, or appraising of residential real property.

(c) Appraisal Exemption.--Nothing in this title prohibits a person engaged in the business of furnishing appraisals of real property to take into consideration factors other than race, color, religion, national origin, sex, handicap, or familial status.

Sec. 806. [42 U.S.C. 3606] Discrimination in provision of brokerage services

After December 31, 1968, it shall be unlawful to deny any person access to or membership or participation in any multiple-listing service, real estate brokers' organization or other service, organization, or facility relating to the business of selling or renting dwellings, or to discriminate against him in the terms or conditions of such access, membership, or participation, on account of race, color, religion, sex, handicap, familial status, or national origin.

Sec. 807. [42 U.S.C. 3607] Religious organization or private club exemption

(a) Nothing in this subchapter shall prohibit a religious organization, association, or society, or any nonprofit institution or organization operated, supervised or controlled by or in conjunction with a religious organization, association, or society, from limiting the sale, rental or occupancy of dwellings which it owns or operates for other than a commercial purpose to persons of the same religion, or from giving preference to such persons, unless membership in such religion is restricted on account of race, color, or national origin. Nor shall anything in this subchapter prohibit a private club not in fact open to the public, which as an incident to its primary purpose or purposes provides lodgings which it owns or operates for other than a commercial purpose, from limiting the rental or occupancy of such lodgings to its members or from giving preference to its members.

(b)

(1) Nothing in this title limits the applicability of any reasonable local, State, or Federal restrictions regarding the maximum number of occupants permitted to occupy a dwelling. Nor does any provision in this title regarding familial status apply with respect to housing

for older persons.

(2) As used in this section "housing for older persons" means housing --

(A) provided under any State or Federal program that the Secretary determines is specifically designed and operated to assist elderly persons (as defined in the State or Federal program); or

(B) intended for, and solely occupied by, persons 62 years of age or older; or

(C) intended and operated for occupancy by persons 55 years of age or older, and--

(i) at least 80 percent of the occupied units are occupied by at least one person who is 55 years of age or older;

(ii) the housing facility or community publishes and adheres to policies and procedures that demonstrate the intent required under this subparagraph; and

(iii) the housing facility or community complies with rules issued by the Secretary for verification of occupancy, which shall--

(I) provide for verification by reliable surveys and affidavits; and

(II) include examples of the types of policies and procedures relevant to a determination of compliance with the requirement of clause (ii). Such surveys and affidavits shall be admissible in administrative and judicial proceedings for the purposes of such verification.

(3) Housing shall not fail to meet the requirements for housing for older persons by reason of:

(A) persons residing in such housing as of the date of enactment of this Act who do not meet the age requirements of subsections (2)(B) or (C): **Provided**, That new occupants of such housing meet the age requirements of sections (2)(B) or (C); or

(B) unoccupied units: **Provided**, That such units are reserved for occupancy by persons who meet the age requirements of subsections (2)(B) or (C).

(4) Nothing in this title prohibits conduct against a person because such person has been convicted by any court of competent jurisdiction of the illegal manufacture or distribution of a controlled substance as defined in section 102 of the Controlled Substances Act (21 U.S.C. 802).

(5)

(A) A person shall not be held personally liable for monetary damages for a violation of this title if such person reasonably relied, in good faith, on the application of the exemption under this subsection relating to housing for older persons.

(B) For the purposes of this paragraph, a person may only show good faith reliance on the application of the exemption by showing that--

(i) such person has no actual knowledge that the facility or community is not, or will not be, eligible for such exemption; and

(ii) the facility or community has stated formally, in writing, that the facility or community complies with the requirements for such exemption.

Sec. 808. [42 U.S.C. 3608] Administration

(a) Authority and responsibility

The authority and responsibility for administering this Act shall be in the Secretary of Housing and Urban Development.

(b) Assistant Secretary

The Department of Housing and Urban Development shall be provided an additional Assistant Secretary.

(c) Delegation of authority; appointment of administrative law judges; location of conciliation meetings; administrative review

The Secretary may delegate any of his functions, duties and power to employees of the Department of Housing and Urban Development or to boards of such employees, including functions, duties, and powers with respect to investigating, conciliating, hearing, determining, ordering, certifying, reporting, or otherwise acting as to any work, business, or matter under this subchapter. The person to whom such delegations are made with respect to hearing functions, duties, and powers shall be appointed and shall serve in the Department of Housing and Urban Development in compliance with sections 3105, 3344, 5372, and 7521 of title 5 [of the United States Code]. Insofar as possible, conciliation meetings shall be held in the cities or other localities where the discriminatory housing practices allegedly occurred. The Secretary shall by rule prescribe such rights of appeal from the decisions of his administrative law judges to other administrative law judges or to other officers in the Department, to boards of officers or to himself, as shall be appropriate and in accordance with law.

(d) Cooperation of Secretary and executive departments and agencies in administration of housing and urban development programs and activities to further fair housing purposes

All executive departments and agencies shall administer their programs and activities relating to housing and urban development (including any Federal agency having regulatory or supervisory authority over financial institutions) in a manner affirmatively to further the purposes of this subchapter and shall cooperate with the Secretary to further such purposes.

(e) Functions of Secretary

The Secretary of Housing and Urban Development shall--

(1) make studies with respect to the nature and extent of discriminatory housing practices in representative communities, urban, suburban, and rural, throughout the United States;

(2) publish and disseminate reports, recommendations, and information derived from such

studies, including an annual report to the Congress--

> (A) specifying the nature and extent of progress made nationally in eliminating discriminatory housing practices and furthering the purposes of this title, obstacles remaining to achieving equal housing opportunity, and recommendations for further legislative or executive action; and

> (B) containing tabulations of the number of instances (and the reasons therefor) in the preceding year in which--

>> (i) investigations are not completed as required by section 810(a)(1)(B);

>> (ii) determinations are not made within the time specified in section 810(g); and

>> (iii) hearings are not commenced or findings and conclusions are not made as required by section 812(g);

(3) cooperate with and render technical assistance to Federal, State, local, and other public or private agencies, organizations, and institutions which are formulating or carrying on programs to prevent or eliminate discriminatory housing practices;

(4) cooperate with and render such technical and other assistance to the Community Relations Service as may be appropriate to further its activities in preventing or eliminating discriminatory housing practices;

(5) administer the programs and activities relating to housing and urban development in a manner affirmatively to further the policies of this subchapter; and

(6) annually report to the Congress, and make available to the public, data on the race, color, religion, sex, national origin, age, handicap, and family characteristics of persons and households who are applicants for, participants in, or beneficiaries or potential beneficiaries of, programs administered by the Department to the extent such characteristics are within the coverage of the provisions of law and Executive orders referred to in subsection (f) which apply to such programs (and in order to develop the data to be included and made available to the public under this subsection, the Secretary shall, without regard to any other provision of law, collect such information relating to those characteristics as the Secretary determines to be necessary or appropriate).

(f) The provisions of law and Executive orders to which subsection (e)(6) applies are--

> (1) title VI of the Civil Rights Act of 1964;

> (2) title VIII of the Civil Rights Act of 1968;

> (3) section 504 of the Rehabilitation Act of 1973;

> (4) the Age Discrimination Act of 1975;

> (5) the Equal Credit Opportunity Act;

(6) section 1978 of the Revised Statutes (42 U.S.C. 1982);

(7) section 8(a) of the Small Business Act;

(8) section 527 of the National Housing Act;

(9) section 109 of the Housing and Community Development Act of 1974;

(10) section 3 of the Housing and Urban Development Act of 1968;

(11) Executive Orders 11063, 11246, 11625, 12250, 12259, and 12432; and

(12) any other provision of law which the Secretary specifies by publication in the Federal Register for the purpose of this subsection.

Sec. 808a. [42 U.S.C. 3608a] Collection of certain data

(a) In general

To assess the extent of compliance with Federal fair housing requirements (including the requirements established under title VI of Public Law 88-352 [42 U.S.C.A. {2000d et seq.] and title VIII of Public Law 90-284 [42 U.S.C.A. {3601 et seq.]), the Secretary of Housing and Urban Development and the Secretary of Agriculture shall each collect, not less than annually, data on the racial and ethnic characteristics of persons eligible for, assisted, or otherwise benefiting under each community development, housing assistance, and mortgage and loan insurance and guarantee program administered by such Secretary. Such data shall be collected on a building by building basis if the Secretary involved determines such collection to be appropriate.

(b) Reports to Congress

The Secretary of Housing and Urban Development and the Secretary of Agriculture shall each include in the annual report of such Secretary to the Congress a summary and evaluation of the data collected by such Secretary under subsection (a) of this section during the preceding year.

Sec. 809. [42 U.S.C. 3609] Education and conciliation; conferences and consultations; reports

Immediately after April 11, 1968, the Secretary shall commence such educational and conciliatory activities as in his judgment will further the purposes of this subchapter. He shall call conferences of persons in the housing industry and other interested parties to acquaint them with the provisions of this subchapter and his suggested means of implementing it, and shall endeavor with their advice to work out programs of voluntary compliance and of enforcement. He may pay per diem, travel, and transportation expenses for persons attending such conferences as provided in section 5703 of Title 5. He shall consult with State and local officials and other interested parties to learn the extent, if any, to which housing discrimination exists in their State or locality, and whether and how State or local enforcement programs might be utilized to combat such discrimination in connection with or in place of, the Secretary's enforcement of this subchapter. The Secretary shall issue reports on such conferences and consultations as he deems appropriate.

Sec. 810. [42 U.S.C. 3610] Administrative Enforcement; Preliminary Matters

(a) Complaints and Answers. --

   (1)

      (A)

(i) An aggrieved person may, not later than one year after an alleged discriminatory housing practice has occurred or terminated, file a complaint with the Secretary alleging such discriminatory housing practice. The Secretary, on the Secretary's own initiative, may also file such a complaint.

(ii) Such complaints shall be in writing and shall contain such information and be in such form as the Secretary requires.

(iii) The Secretary may also investigate housing practices to determine whether a complaint should be brought under this section.

      (B) Upon the filing of such a complaint--

(i) the Secretary shall serve notice upon the aggrieved person acknowledging such filing and advising the aggrieved person of the time limits and choice of forums provided under this title;

(ii) the Secretary shall, not later than 10 days after such filing or the identification of an additional respondent under paragraph (2), serve on the respondent a notice identifying the alleged discriminatory housing practice and advising such respondent of the procedural rights and obligations of respondents under this title, together with a copy of the original complaint;

(iii) each respondent may file, not later than 10 days after receipt of notice from the Secretary, an answer to such complaint; and

(iv) the Secretary shall make an investigation of the alleged discriminatory housing practice and complete such investigation within 100 days after the filing of the complaint (or, when the Secretary takes further action under subsection (f)(2) with respect to a complaint, within 100 days after the commencement of such further action), unless it is impracticable to do so.

      (C) If the Secretary is unable to complete the investigation within 100 days after the filing of the complaint (or, when the Secretary takes further action under subsection (f)(2) with respect to a complaint, within 100 days after the commencement of such further action), the Secretary shall notify the complainant and respondent in writing of the reasons for not doing so.

      (D) Complaints and answers shall be under oath or affirmation, and may be reasonably and fairly amended at any time.

   (2)

      (A) A person who is not named as a respondent in a complaint, but who is identified as a respondent in the course of investigation, may be joined as an additional or substitute respondent upon written notice, under paragraph (1), to such person, from the Secretary.

(B) Such notice, in addition to meeting the requirements of paragraph (1), shall explain the basis for the Secretary's belief that the person to whom the notice is addressed is properly joined as a respondent.

(b) Investigative Report and Conciliation. --

(1) During the period beginning with the filing of such complaint and ending with the filing of a charge or a dismissal by the Secretary, the Secretary shall, to the extent feasible, engage in conciliation with respect to such complaint.

(2) A conciliation agreement arising out of such conciliation shall be an agreement between the respondent and the complainant, and shall be subject to approval by the Secretary.

(3) A conciliation agreement may provide for binding arbitration of the dispute arising from the complaint. Any such arbitration that results from a conciliation agreement may award appropriate relief, including monetary relief.

(4) Each conciliation agreement shall be made public unless the complainant and respondent otherwise agree and the Secretary determines that disclosure is not required to further the purposes of this title.

(5)

(A) At the end of each investigation under this section, the Secretary shall prepare a final investigative report containing--

(i) the names and dates of contacts with witnesses;

(ii) a summary and the dates of correspondence and other contacts with the aggrieved person and the respondent;

(iii) a summary description of other pertinent records;

(iv) a summary of witness statements; and

(v) answers to interrogatories.

(B) A final report under this paragraph may be amended if additional evidence is later discovered.

(c) Failure to Comply With Conciliation Agreement. -- Whenever the Secretary has reasonable cause to believe that a respondent has breached a conciliation agreement, the Secretary shall refer the matter to the Attorney General with a recommendation that a civil action be filed under section 814 for the enforcement of such agreement.

(d) Prohibitions and Requirements With Respect to Disclosure of Information. --

(1) Nothing said or done in the course of conciliation under this title may be made public or used as evidence in a subsequent proceeding under this title without the written consent of the persons concerned.

(2) Notwithstanding paragraph (1), the Secretary shall make available to the aggrieved person and the respondent, at any time, upon request following completion of the

Secretary's investigation, information derived from an investigation and any final investigative report relating to that investigation.

(e) Prompt Judicial Action. --

(1) If the Secretary concludes at any time following the filing of a complaint that prompt judicial action is necessary to carry out the purposes of this title, the Secretary may authorize a civil action for appropriate temporary or preliminary relief pending final disposition of the complaint under this section. Upon receipt of such authorization, the Attorney General shall promptly commence and maintain such an action. Any temporary restraining order or other order granting preliminary or temporary relief shall be issued in accordance with the Federal Rules of Civil Procedure. The commencement of a civil action under this subsection does not affect the initiation or continuation of administrative proceedings under this section and section 812 of this title.

(2) Whenever the Secretary has reason to believe that a basis may exist for the commencement of proceedings against any respondent under section 814(a) and 814(c) or for proceedings by any governmental licensing or supervisory authorities, the Secretary shall transmit the information upon which such belief is based to the Attorney General, or to such authorities, as the case may be.

(f) Referral for State or Local Proceedings. --

(1) Whenever a complaint alleges a discriminatory housing practice--

(A) within the jurisdiction of a State or local public agency; and

(B) as to which such agency has been certified by the Secretary under this subsection; the Secretary shall refer such complaint to that certified agency before taking any action with respect to such complaint.

(2) Except with the consent of such certified agency, the Secretary, after that referral is made, shall take no further action with respect to such complaint unless--

(A) the certified agency has failed to commence proceedings with respect to the complaint before the end of the 30th day after the date of such referral;

(B) the certified agency, having so commenced such proceedings, fails to carry forward such proceedings with reasonable promptness; or

(C) the Secretary determines that the certified agency no longer qualifies for certification under this subsection with respect to the relevant jurisdiction.

(3)

(A) The Secretary may certify an agency under this subsection only if the Secretary determines that--

(i) the substantive rights protected by such agency in the jurisdiction with respect to which certification is to be made;

(ii) the procedures followed by such agency;

(iii) the remedies available to such agency; and

(iv) the availability of judicial review of such agency's action;

are substantially equivalent to those created by and under this title.

(B) Before making such certification, the Secretary shall take into account the current practices and past performance, if any, of such agency.

(4) During the period which begins on the date of the enactment of the Fair Housing Amendments Act of 1988 and ends 40 months after such date, each agency certified (including an agency certified for interim referrals pursuant to 24 CFR 115.11, unless such agency is subsequently denied recognition under 24 CFR 115.7) for the purposes of this title on the day before such date shall for the purposes of this subsection be considered certified under this subsection with respect to those matters for which such agency was certified on that date. If the Secretary determines in an individual case that an agency has not been able to meet the certification requirements within this 40-month period due to exceptional circumstances, such as the infrequency of legislative sessions in that jurisdiction, the Secretary may extend such period by not more than 8 months.

(5) Not less frequently than every 5 years, the Secretary shall determine whether each agency certified under this subsection continues to qualify for certification. The Secretary shall take appropriate action with respect to any agency not so qualifying.

(g) Reasonable Cause Determination and Effect. --

(1) The Secretary shall, within 100 days after the filing of the complaint (or, when the Secretary takes further action under subsection (f)(2) with respect to a complaint, within 100 days after the commencement of such further action), determine based on the facts whether reasonable cause exists to believe that a discriminatory housing practice has occurred or is about to occur, unless it is impracticable to do so, or unless the Secretary has approved a conciliation agreement with respect to the complaint. If the Secretary is unable to make the determination within 100 days after the filing of the complaint (or, when the Secretary takes further action under subsection (f)(2) with respect to a complaint, within 100 days after the commencement of such further action), the Secretary shall notify the complainant and respondent in writing of the reasons for not doing so.

(2)

(A) If the Secretary determines that reasonable cause exists to believe that a discriminatory housing practice has occurred or is about to occur, the Secretary shall, except as provided in subparagraph (C), immediately issue a charge on behalf of the aggrieved person, for further proceedings under section 812.

(B) Such charge--

(i) shall consist of a short and plain statement of the facts upon which the Secretary has found reasonable cause to believe that a discriminatory housing practice has occurred or is about to occur;

(ii) shall be based on the final investigative report; and

(iii) need not be limited to the facts or grounds alleged in the complaint filed under section 810(a).

(C) If the Secretary determines that the matter involves the legality of any State or local zoning or other land use law or ordinance, the Secretary shall immediately refer the matter to the Attorney General for appropriate action under section 814, instead of issuing such charge.

(3) If the Secretary determines that no reasonable cause exists to believe that a discriminatory housing practice has occurred or is about to occur, the Secretary shall promptly dismiss the complaint. The Secretary shall make public disclosure of each such dismissal.

(4) The Secretary may not issue a charge under this section regarding an alleged discriminatory housing practice after the beginning of the trial of a civil action commenced by the aggrieved party under an Act of Congress or a State law, seeking relief with respect to that discriminatory housing practice.

(h) Service of Copies of Charge. -- After the Secretary issues a charge under this section, the Secretary shall cause a copy thereof, together with information as to how to make an election under section 812(a) and the effect of such an election, to be served--

(1) on each respondent named in such charge, together with a notice of opportunity for a hearing at a time and place specified in the notice, unless that election is made; and

(2) on each aggrieved person on whose behalf the complaint was filed.

Sec. 811. [42 U.S.C. 3611] Subpoenas; Giving of Evidence

(a) In General. -- The Secretary may, in accordance with this subsection, issue subpoenas and order discovery in aid of investigations and hearings under this title. Such subpoenas and discovery may be ordered to the same extent and subject to the same limitations as would apply if the subpoenas or discovery were ordered or served in aid of a civil action in the United States district court for the district in which the investigation is taking place.

(b) Witness Fees. -- Witnesses summoned by a subpoena under this title shall be entitled to same witness and mileage fees as witnesses in proceedings in United States district courts. Fees payable to a witness summoned by a subpoena issued at the request of a party shall be paid by that party or, where a party is unable to pay the fees, by the Secretary.

(c) Criminal Penalties. --

(1) Any person who willfully fails or neglects to attend and testify or to answer any lawful inquiry or to produce records, documents, or other evidence, if it is in such person's power to do so, in obedience to the subpoena or other lawful order under subsection (a), shall be fined not more than $100,000 or imprisoned not more than one year, or both.

(2) Any person who, with intent thereby to mislead another person in any proceeding under

this title--

    (A) makes or causes to be made any false entry or statement of fact in any report, account, record, or other document produced pursuant to subpoena or other lawful order under subsection (a);

    (B) willfully neglects or fails to make or to cause to be made full, true, and correct entries in such reports, accounts, records, or other documents; or

    (C) willfully mutilates, alters, or by any other means falsifies any documentary evidence;

        shall be fined not more than $100,000 or imprisoned not more than one year, or both.

Sec. 812. [42 U.S.C. 3612] Enforcement by Secretary

(a) Election of Judicial Determination. -- When a charge is filed under section 810, a complainant, a respondent, or an aggrieved person on whose behalf the complaint was filed, may elect to have the claims asserted in that charge decided in a civil action under subsection (o) in lieu of a hearing under subsection (b). The election must be made not later than 20 days after the receipt by the electing person of service under section 810(h) or, in the case of the Secretary, not later than 20 days after such service. The person making such election shall give notice of doing so to the Secretary and to all other complainants and respondents to whom the charge relates.

(b) Administrative Law Judge Hearing in Absence of Election. -- If an election is not made under subsection (a) with respect to a charge filed under section 810, the Secretary shall provide an opportunity for a hearing on the record with respect to a charge issued under section 810. The Secretary shall delegate the conduct of a hearing under this section to an administrative law judge appointed under section 3105 of title 5, United States Code. The administrative law judge shall conduct the hearing at a place in the vicinity in which the discriminatory housing practice is alleged to have occurred or to be about to occur.

(c) Rights of Parties. -- At a hearing under this section, each party may appear in person, be represented by counsel, present evidence, cross-examine witnesses, and obtain the issuance of subpoenas under section 811. Any aggrieved person may intervene as a party in the proceeding. The Federal Rules of Evidence apply to the presentation of evidence in such hearing as they would in a civil action in a United States district court.

(d) Expedited Discovery and Hearing. --

    (1) Discovery in administrative proceedings under this section shall be conducted as expeditiously and inexpensively as possible, consistent with the need of all parties to obtain relevant evidence.

    (2) A hearing under this section shall be conducted as expeditiously and inexpensively as possible, consistent with the needs and rights of the parties to obtain a fair hearing and a complete record.

    (3) The Secretary shall, not later than 180 days after the date of enactment of this

subsection, issue rules to implement this subsection.

(e) Resolution of Charge. -- Any resolution of a charge before a final order under this section shall require the consent of the aggrieved person on whose behalf the charge is issued.

(f) Effect of Trial of Civil Action on Administrative Proceedings. -- An administrative law judge may not continue administrative proceedings under this section regarding any alleged discriminatory housing practice after the beginning of the trial of a civil action commenced by the aggrieved party under an Act of Congress or a State law, seeking relief with respect to that discriminatory housing practice.

(g) Hearings, Findings and Conclusions, and Order. -- (

(1) The administrative law judge shall commence the hearing under this section no later than 120 days following the issuance of the charge, unless it is impracticable to do so. If the administrative law judge is unable to commence the hearing within 120 days after the issuance of the charge, the administrative law judge shall notify the Secretary, the aggrieved person on whose behalf the charge was filed, and the respondent, in writing of the reasons for not doing so.

(2) The administrative law judge shall make findings of fact and conclusions of law within 60 days after the end of the hearing under this section, unless it is impracticable to do so. If the administrative law judge is unable to make findings of fact and conclusions of law within such period, or any succeeding 60-day period thereafter, the administrative law judge shall notify the Secretary, the aggrieved person on whose behalf the charge was filed, and the respondent, in writing of the reasons for not doing so.

(3) If the administrative law judge finds that a respondent has engaged or is about to engage in a discriminatory housing practice, such administrative law judge shall promptly issue an order for such relief as may be appropriate, which may include actual damages suffered by the aggrieved person and injunctive or other equitable relief. Such order may, to vindicate the public interest, assess a civil penalty against the respondent--

(A) in an amount not exceeding $11,000 if the respondent has not been adjudged to have committed any prior discriminatory housing practice;

(B) in an amount not exceeding $27,500 if the respondent has been adjudged to have committed one other discriminatory housing practice during the 5-year period ending on the date of the filing of this charge; and

(C) in an amount not exceeding $55,000 if the respondent has been adjudged to have committed 2 or more discriminatory housing practices during the 7-year period ending on the date of the filing of this charge;

except that if the acts constituting the discriminatory housing practice that is the object of the charge are committed by the same natural person who has been previously adjudged to have committed acts constituting a discriminatory housing practice, then the civil penalties set forth in subparagraphs (B) and (C) may be imposed without regard to the period of time within which any subsequent discriminatory housing practice occurred.

(4) No such order shall affect any contract, sale, encumbrance, or lease consummated before the issuance of such order and involving a bona fide purchaser, encumbrancer, or tenant without actual notice of the charge filed under this title.

(5) In the case of an order with respect to a discriminatory housing practice that occurred in the course of a business subject to a licensing or regulation by a governmental agency, the Secretary shall, not later than 30 days after the date of the issuance of such order (or, if such order is judicially reviewed, 30 days after such order is in substance affirmed upon such review)--

(A) send copies of the findings of fact, conclusions of law, and the order, to that governmental agency; and

(B) recommend to that governmental agency appropriate disciplinary action (including, where appropriate, the suspension or revocation of the license of the respondent).

(6) In the case of an order against a respondent against whom another order was issued within the preceding 5 years under this section, the Secretary shall send a copy of each such order to the Attorney General.

(7) If the administrative law judge finds that the respondent has not engaged or is not about to engage in a discriminatory housing practice, as the case may be, such administrative law judge shall enter an order dismissing the charge. The Secretary shall make public disclosure of each such dismissal.

(h) Review by Secretary; Service of Final Order. --

(1) The Secretary may review any finding, conclusion, or order issued under subsection (g). Such review shall be completed not later than 30 days after the finding, conclusion, or order is so issued; otherwise the finding, conclusion, or order becomes final.

(2) The Secretary shall cause the findings of fact and conclusions of law made with respect to any final order for relief under this section, together with a copy of such order, to be served on each aggrieved person and each respondent in the proceeding.

(i) Judicial Review. --

(1) Any party aggrieved by a final order for relief under this section granting or denying in whole or in part the relief sought may obtain a review of such order under chapter 158 of title 28, United States Code.

(2) Notwithstanding such chapter, venue of the proceeding shall be in the judicial circuit in which the discriminatory housing practice is alleged to have occurred, and filing of the petition for review shall be not later than 30 days after the order is entered.

(j) Court Enforcement of Administrative Order Upon Petition by Secretary. --

(1) The Secretary may petition any United States court of appeals for the circuit in which the discriminatory housing practice is alleged to have occurred or in which any respondent

resides or transacts business for the enforcement of the order of the administrative law judge and for appropriate temporary relief or restraining order, by filing in such court a written petition praying that such order be enforced and for appropriate temporary relief or restraining order.

(2) The Secretary shall file in court with the petition the record in the proceeding. A copy of such petition shall be forthwith transmitted by the clerk of the court to the parties to the proceeding before the administrative law judge.

(k) Relief Which May Be Granted. --

(1) Upon the filing of a petition under subsection (i) or (j), the court may--

(A) grant to the petitioner, or any other party, such temporary relief, restraining order, or other order as the court deems just and proper;

(B) affirm, modify, or set aside, in whole or in part, the order, or remand the order for further proceedings; and

(C) enforce such order to the extent that such order is affirmed or modified.

(2) Any party to the proceeding before the administrative law judge may intervene in the court of appeals.

(3) No objection not made before the administrative law judge shall be considered by the court, unless the failure or neglect to urge such objection is excused because of extraordinary circumstances.

(l) Enforcement Decree in Absence of Petition for Review. -- If no petition for review is filed under subsection (i) before the expiration of 45 days after the date the administrative law judge's order is entered, the administrative law judge's findings of fact and order shall be conclusive in connection with any petition for enforcement--

(1) which is filed by the Secretary under subsection (j) after the end of such day; or

(2) under subsection (m).

(m) Court Enforcement of Administrative Order Upon Petition of Any Person Entitled to Relief. -- If before the expiration of 60 days after the date the administrative law judge's order is entered, no petition for review has been filed under subsection (i), and the Secretary has not sought enforcement of the order under subsection (j), any person entitled to relief under the order may petition for a decree enforcing the order in the United States court of appeals for the circuit in which the discriminatory housing practice is alleged to have occurred.

(n) Entry of Decree. -- The clerk of the court of appeals in which a petition for enforcement is filed under subsection (1) or (m) shall forthwith enter a decree enforcing the order and shall transmit a copy of such decree to the Secretary, the respondent named in the petition, and to any other parties to the proceeding before the administrative law judge.

(o) Civil Action for Enforcement When Election Is Made for Such Civil Action. --

(1) If an election is made under subsection (a), the Secretary shall authorize, and not later than 30 days after the election is made the Attorney General shall commence and maintain, a civil action on behalf of the aggrieved person in a United States district court seeking relief under this subsection. Venue for such civil action shall be determined under chapter 87 of title 28, United States Code.

(2) Any aggrieved person with respect to the issues to be determined in a civil action under this subsection may intervene as of right in that civil action.

(3) In a civil action under this subsection, if the court finds that a discriminatory housing practice has occurred or is about to occur, the court may grant as relief any relief which a court could grant with respect to such discriminatory housing practice in a civil action under section 813. Any relief so granted that would accrue to an aggrieved person in a civil action commenced by that aggrieved person under section 813 shall also accrue to that aggrieved person in a civil action under this subsection. If monetary relief is sought for the benefit of an aggrieved person who does not intervene in the civil action, the court shall not award such relief if that aggrieved person has not complied with discovery orders entered by the court.

(p) Attorney's Fees. -- In any administrative proceeding brought under this section, or any court proceeding arising therefrom, or any civil action under section 812, the administrative law judge or the court, as the case may be, in its discretion, may allow the prevailing party, other than the United States, a reasonable attorney's fee and costs. The United States shall be liable for such fees and costs to the extent provided by section 504 of title 5, United States Code, or by section 2412 of title 28, United States Code.

Sec. 813. [42 U.S.C. 3613] Enforcement by Private Persons

(a) Civil Action. --

(1)

(A) An aggrieved person may commence a civil action in an appropriate United States district court or State court not later than 2 years after the occurrence or the termination of an alleged discriminatory housing practice, or the breach of a conciliation agreement entered into under this title, whichever occurs last, to obtain appropriate relief with respect to such discriminatory housing practice or breach.

(B) The computation of such 2-year period shall not include any time during which an administrative proceeding under this title was pending with respect to a complaint or charge under this title based upon such discriminatory housing practice. This subparagraph does not apply to actions arising from a breach of a conciliation agreement.

(2) An aggrieved person may commence a civil action under this subsection whether or not a complaint has been filed under section 810(a) and without regard to the status of any such complaint, but if the Secretary or a State or local agency has obtained a conciliation agreement with the consent of an aggrieved person, no action may be filed under this subsection by such aggrieved person with respect to the alleged discriminatory housing practice which forms the basis for such complaint except for the purpose of enforcing the

terms of such an agreement.

(3) An aggrieved person may not commence a civil action under this subsection with respect to an alleged discriminatory housing practice which forms the basis of a charge issued by the Secretary if an administrative law judge has commenced a hearing on the record under this title with respect to such charge.

(b) Appointment of Attorney by Court. -- Upon application by a person alleging a discriminatory housing practice or a person against whom such a practice is alleged, the court may--

(1) appoint an attorney for such person; or

(2) authorize the commencement or continuation of a civil action under subsection (a) without the payment of fees, costs, or security, if in the opinion of the court such person is financially unable to bear the costs of such action.

(c) Relief Which May Be Granted. --

(1) In a civil action under subsection (a), if the court finds that a discriminatory housing practice has occurred or is about to occur, the court may award to the plaintiff actual and punitive damages, and subject to subsection (d), may grant as relief, as the court deems appropriate, any permanent or temporary injunction, temporary restraining order, or other order (including an order enjoining the defendant from engaging in such practice or ordering such affirmative action as may be appropriate).

(2) In a civil action under subsection (a), the court, in its discretion, may allow the prevailing party, other than the United States, a reasonable attorney's fee and costs. The United States shall be liable for such fees and costs to the same extent as a private person.

(d) Effect on Certain Sales, Encumbrances, and Rentals. -- Relief granted under this section shall not affect any contract, sale, encumbrance, or lease consummated before the granting of such relief and involving a bona fide purchaser, encumbrancer, or tenant, without actual notice of the filing of a complaint with the Secretary or civil action under this title.

(e) Intervention by Attorney General. -- Upon timely application, the Attorney General may intervene in such civil action, if the Attorney General certifies that the case is of general public importance. Upon such intervention the Attorney General may obtain such relief as would be available to the Attorney General under section 814(e) in a civil action to which such section applies.

Sec. 814. [42 U.S.C. 3614] Enforcement by the Attorney General

(a) Pattern or Practice Cases. -- Whenever the Attorney General has reasonable cause to believe that any person or group of persons is engaged in a pattern or practice of resistance to the full enjoyment of any of the rights granted by this title, or that any group of persons has been denied any of the rights granted by this title and such denial raises an issue of general public importance, the Attorney General may commence a civil action in any appropriate United States district court.

(b) On Referral of Discriminatory Housing Practice or Conciliation Agreement for Enforcement. --

(1)

 (A) The Attorney General may commence a civil action in any appropriate United States district court for appropriate relief with respect to a discriminatory housing practice referred to the Attorney General by the Secretary under section 810(g).

 (B) A civil action under this paragraph may be commenced not later than the expiration of 18 months after the date of the occurrence or the termination of the alleged discriminatory housing practice.

(2)

 (A) The Attorney General may commence a civil action in any appropriate United States district court for appropriate relief with respect to breach of a conciliation agreement referred to the Attorney General by the Secretary under section 810(c).

 (B) A civil action may be commenced under this paragraph not later than the expiration of 90 days after the referral of the alleged breach under section 810(c).

(c) Enforcement of Subpoenas. -- The Attorney General, on behalf of the Secretary, or other party at whose request a subpoena is issued, under this title, may enforce such subpoena in appropriate proceedings in the United States district court for the district in which the person to whom the subpoena was addressed resides, was served, or transacts business.

(d) Relief Which May Be Granted in Civil Actions Under Subsections (a) and (b). --

 (1) In a civil action under subsection (a) or (b), the court--

  (A) may award such preventive relief, including a permanent or temporary injunction, restraining order, or other order against the person responsible for a violation of this title as is necessary to assure the full enjoyment of the rights granted by this title;

  (B) may award such other relief as the court deems appropriate, including monetary damages to persons aggrieved; and

  (C) may, to vindicate the public interest, assess a civil penalty against the respondent--

   (i) in an amount not exceeding $55,000, for a first violation; and

   (ii) in an amount not exceeding $110,000, for any subsequent violation.

 (2) In a civil action under this section, the court, in its discretion, may allow the prevailing party, other than the United States, a reasonable attorney's fee and costs. The United States shall be liable for such fees and costs to the extent provided by section 2412 of title 28, United States Code.

(e) Intervention in Civil Actions. -- Upon timely application, any person may intervene in a civil action commenced by the Attorney General under subsection (a) or (b) which involves an alleged discriminatory housing practice with respect to which such person is an aggrieved person or a conciliation agreement to which such person is a party. The court may grant such appropriate relief to any such intervening party as is authorized to be granted to a plaintiff in a civil action under section 813.

Sec. 814a. Incentives for Self-Testing and Self-Correction

(a) Privileged Information. --

(1) Conditions For Privilege. -- A report or result of a self-test (as that term is defined by regulation of the Secretary) shall be considered to be privileged under paragraph (2) if any person-

(A) conducts, or authorizes an independent third party to conduct, a self- test of any aspect of a residential real estate related lending transaction of that person, or any part of that transaction, in order to determine the level or effectiveness of compliance with this title by that person; and

(B) has identified any possible violation of this title by that person and has taken, or is taking, appropriate corrective action to address any such possible violation.

(2) Privileged Self-Test. -- If a person meets the conditions specified in subparagraphs (A) and (B) of paragraph (1) with respect to a self-test described in that paragraph, any report or results of that self-test-

(A) shall be privileged; and

(B) may not be obtained or used by any applicant, department, or agency in any --

(i) proceeding or civil action in which one or more violations of this title are alleged; or

(ii) examination or investigation relating to compliance with this title.

(b) Results of Self-Testing. --

(1) In General. -- No provision of this section may be construed to prevent an aggrieved person, complainant, department, or agency from obtaining or using a report or results of any self-test in any proceeding or civil action in which a violation of this title is alleged, or in any examination or investigation of compliance with this title if --

(A) the person to whom the self-test relates or any person with lawful access to the report or the results --

(i) voluntarily releases or discloses all, or any part of, the report or results to the aggrieved person, complainant, department, or agency, or to the general public; or

(ii) refers to or describes the report or results as a defense to charges of violations of this title against the person to whom the self-test relates; or

(B) the report or results are sought in conjunction with an adjudication or admission of a violation of this title for the sole purpose of determining an appropriate penalty or remedy.

(2) Disclosure for Determination of Penalty or Remedy. -- Any report or results of a self-test that are disclosed for the purpose specified in paragraph (1)(B) --

(A) shall be used only for the particular proceeding in which the adjudication or admission referred to in paragraph (1)(B) is made; and

(B) may not be used in any other action or proceeding.

(c) Adjudication. -- An aggrieved person, complainant, department, or agency that challenges a privilege asserted under this section may seek a determination of the existence and application of that privilege in --

(1) a court of competent jurisdiction; or

(2) an administrative law proceeding with appropriate jurisdiction.

(2) Regulations. --

(A) In General. -- Not later than 6 months after the date of enactment of this Act, in consultation with the Board and after providing notice and an opportunity for public comment, the Secretary of Housing and Urban Development shall prescribe final regulations to implement section 814A of the Fair Housing Act, as added by this section.

(B) Self-Test. --

(i) Definition. -- The regulations prescribed by the Secretary under subparagraph (A) shall include a definition of the term "self-test" for purposes of section 814A of the Fair Housing Act, as added by this section.

(ii) Requirement for Self-Test. -- The regulations prescribed by the Secretary under subparagraph (A) shall specify that a self-test shall be sufficiently extensive to constitute a determination of the level and effectiveness of the compliance by a person engaged in residential real estate related lending activities with the Fair Housing Act.

(iii) Substantial Similarity to Certain Equal Credit Opportunity Act Regulations. -- The regulations prescribed under subparagraph (A) shall be substantially similar to the regulations prescribed by the Board to carry out section 704A of the Equal Credit Opportunity Act, as added by this section.

(C) Applicability. --

(1) In General. -- Except as provided in paragraph (2), the privilege provided for in section 704a of the Equal Credit Opportunity Act or section 814a of the Fair Housing Act (as those sections are added by this section) shall apply to a

self-test (as that term is defined pursuant to the regulations prescribed under subsection (a)(2) or (b)(2) of this section, as appropriate) conducted before, on, or after the effective date of the regulations prescribed under subsection (a)(2) or (b)(2), as appropriate.

(2) Exception. -- The privilege referred to in paragraph (1) does not apply to such a self-test conducted before the effective date of the regulations prescribed under subsection (a) or (b), as appropriate, if --

(A) before that effective date, a complaint against the creditor or person engaged in residential real estate related lending activities (as the case may be) was --

(i) formally filed in any court of competent jurisdiction; or

(ii) the subject of an ongoing administrative law proceeding;

(B) in the case of section 704a of the Equal Credit Opportunity Act, the creditor has waived the privilege pursuant to subsection (b)(1)(A)(i) of that section; or

(C) in the case of section 814a of the Fair Housing Act, the person engaged in residential real estate related lending activities has waived the privilege pursuant to subsection (b)(1)(A)(i) of that section.

Sec. 815. [42 U.S.C. 3614a] Rules to Implement Title

The Secretary may make rules (including rules for the collection, maintenance, and analysis of appropriate data) to carry out this title. The Secretary shall give public notice and opportunity for comment with respect to all rules made under this section.

Sec. 816. [42 U.S.C. 3615] Effect on State laws

Nothing in this subchapter shall be constructed to invalidate or limit any law of a State or political subdivision of a State, or of any other jurisdiction in which this subchapter shall be effective, that grants, guarantees, or protects the same rights as are granted by this subchapter; but any law of a State, a political subdivision, or other such jurisdiction that purports to require or permit any action that would be a discriminatory housing practice under this subchapter shall to that extent be invalid.

Sec. 817. [42 U.S.C. 3616] Cooperation with State and local agencies administering fair housing laws; utilization of services and personnel; reimbursement; written agreements; publication in

Federal Register

The Secretary may cooperate with State and local agencies charged with the administration of State and local fair housing laws and, with the consent of such agencies, utilize the services of such agencies and their employees and, notwithstanding any other provision of law, may reimburse such agencies and their employees for services rendered to assist him in carrying out this subchapter. In furtherance of such cooperative efforts, the Secretary may enter into written agreements with such State or local agencies. All agreements and terminations thereof shall be published in the Federal Register.

Sec. 818. [42 U.S.C. 3617] Interference, coercion, or intimidation; enforcement by civil action

It shall be unlawful to coerce, intimidate, threaten, or interfere with any person in the exercise or enjoyment of, or on account of his having exercised or enjoyed, or on account of his having aided or encouraged any other person in the exercise or enjoyment of, any right granted or protected by section 803, 804, 805, or 806 of this title.

Sec. 819. [42 U.S.C. 3618] Authorization of appropriations

There are hereby authorized to be appropriated such sums as are necessary to carry out the purposes of this subchapter.

Sec. 820. [42 U.S.C. 3619] Separability of provisions

If any provision of this subchapter or the application thereof to any person or circumstances is held invalid, the remainder of the subchapter and the application of the provision to other persons not similarly situated or to other circumstances shall not be affected thereby.

(Sec. 12 of 1988 Act). [42 U.S.C. 3601 note] Disclaimer of Preemptive Effect on Other Acts

Nothing in the Fair Housing Act as amended by this Act limits any right, procedure, or remedy available under the Constitution or any other Act of the Congress not so amended.

(Sec. 13 of 1988 Act). [42 U.S.C. 3601 note] Effective Date and Initial Rulemaking

(a) Effective Date. -- This Act and the amendments made by this Act shall take effect on the 180th day beginning after the date of the enactment of this Act.

(b) Initial Rulemaking. -- In consultation with other appropriate Federal agencies, the Secretary shall, not later than the 180th day after the date of the enactment of this Act, issue rules to implement title VIII as amended by this Act. The Secretary shall give public notice and opportunity for comment with respect to such rules.

(Sec. 14 of 1988 Act). [42 U.S.C. 3601 note] Separability of Provisions

If any provision of this Act or the application thereof to any person or circumstances is held invalid, the remainder of the Act and the application of the provision to other persons not similarly situated or to other circumstances shall not be affected thereby.

Section 901. (Title IX As Amended) [42 U.S.C. 3631] Violations; bodily injury; death; penalties

Whoever, whether or not acting under color of law, by force or threat of force willfully injures, intimidates or interferes with, or attempts to injure, intimidate or interfere with--

(a) any person because of his race, color, religion, sex, handicap (as such term is defined in section 802 of this Act), familial status (as such term is defined in section 802 of this Act), or national origin and because he is or has been selling, purchasing, renting, financing occupying, or contracting or negotiating for the sale, purchase, rental, financing or occupation of any dwelling, or applying for or participating in any service, organization, or facility relating to the business of selling or renting dwellings; or

Bonus CD-ROM:
The American Tenant Resource Center

System Requirements:

★ **Windows 2000, XP or Vista (with CD-ROM Drive)**

★ **Adobe Reader (Version 7 or Higher - Available as a Free Download)**

★ **Internet Connection (Recommended)**

The enclosed CD-ROM is outfitted with rental forms, agreements and publications, among many other invaluable resources *[some forms and agreements may need to be modified (or amended) to accommodate new or existing laws in your state]*. Each form comes equipped with fields that can be highlighted and then hovered with your mouse for pop-up instructions. You can even personalize each form and agreement with your contact information and logo *[see the illustrations on the following pages]*.

Installation Instructions

Insert the CD into your CD-ROM drive and follow the onscreen instructions. If the installation process does not automatically begin, click the **START** button, then click **RUN** and type in the following: **D:\americantenant.exe** and click **OK** to begin following the onscreen instructions. *(If the location of your CD-ROM begins with a letter other than **D**, you must replace it with the proper drive letter.)*

Terms of Use

All copyrighted forms are provided for your personal use only and may not be redistributed or sold. Note: The contents of this CD-ROM are not intended as a substitute for the advice of an attorney.

How to Personalize a Rental Form

Highlight instructions to delete or replace with your contact information

Everything U Need to Know...

Click here to insert image/logo

Insert a logo or image from your computer to display on the top right of your form

Instructions:
1. Insert your IMAGE
2. Enter 'PROPE
3. REPLACE ALL of this te
4. Click on 'PRINT FORM' when

Application

Applicant Information		
Property address applying for: **1002 Nor_**		
Name:		
Date of birth:	SSN:	
Current address:		
City:		ZIP Code:
Own Re		How long?
Previous		
City:		ZIP Code:
Owned		How long?

Forms with landlord required fields can be completed onscreen before printing

Employment		
Current employer:		
Employer address:		How long?
City:	State	ZIP Code:
Phone:		
Position:		

Your personalized information cannot be saved - so be sure to print multiple copies for future use

Emergency Contac		
Name of a person not residi		
Address:		
City:	State	Phone:
Relationship:		

References		
Name:	Address:	Phone:

The End Result

JOHN Z. DOE RENTAL PROPERTY LLC
2008 Western Avenue
Anytown, USA 12345
PH (555) 555-1212
FX (555) 555-1313

Residential Rental Application

Applicant Information		
Property address applying for: 1002 North Canyon Rd , Unit #3, Anytown, USA 12345		

Name:		
Date of birth:	SSN:	Phone:
Current address:		
City:	State:	ZIP Code:
Own Rent (Please circle)	Monthly payment or rent:	How long?
Previous address:		
City:	State:	ZIP Code:
Owned Rented (Please circle)	Monthly payment or rent:	How long?

Employment Information		
Current employer:		
Employer address:		How long?
City:	State:	ZIP Code:
Phone:	E-mail:	Fax:
Position:	Hourly Salary (Please circle)	Annual income:

Emergency Contact			
Name of a person not residing with you:			
Address:			
City:	State:	ZIP Code:	Phone:
Relationship:			

References		
Name:	Address:	Phone:

Have you ever been convicted of a crime? (yes / no) If so, please explain all offenses including where, when and why:

Have you ever been evicted? (yes / no) If so, please explain where, when and why:

I acknowledge that falsification or omission of any information on this rental application may result in the immediate dismissal or retraction of an offer of tenancy. I hereby voluntarily consent to and authorize the AmerUSA Corporation ("AmerUSA"), acting as the landlord's designated screening organization for the above referenced rental property, to obtain my consumer report and render a credit decision. I further authorize all persons and organizations that may have information relevant to this research to disclose such information to the landlord's authorized agent, AmerUSA. I hereby release the landlord and its authorized agent, AmerUSA, from all claims and liabilities of any nature in connection with this research, results and decision. A photocopy of this authorization will be considered valid. I understand that I have specific prescribed rights as a consumer under the federal Fair Credit Reporting Act ('FCRA') and have received a copy of those rights titled "FCRA Summary of Rights."

Signature of applicant:	Date:

This form provided by USLandlord.com

Index

AMERICAN
FORECLOSURE

Everything U Need to Know...™

about

PREVENTING & BUYING

★ Foreclosure Process

★ Find the Best Deals

★ Finance Options

★ Save Your Home

★ Avoid Scams

★ And Much More...

TREVOR RHODES, CEO OF AMERUSA

Includes ready-to-print real estate forms, foreclosure
prevention resources, free property listings—
and much more!

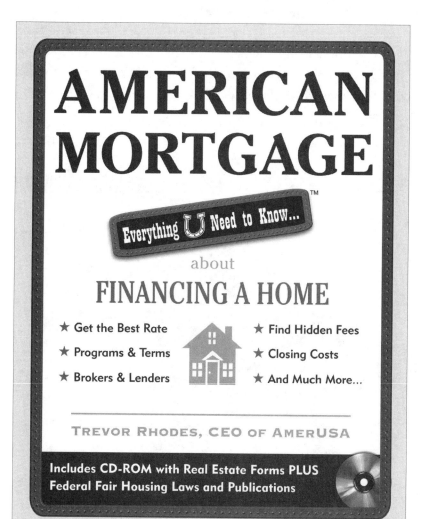

We would like to hear from you!

Please email us your comments or suggestions about *American Tenant* or any other volume from the Everything U Need to Know... series. Whether it's an idea for a new volume or a comment about an existing one, it's always a distinct pleasure to hear what *you* have to say...

feedback@euntk.com